A basic English examination course

steps

TO GCSE SUCCESS

Paul Groves
John Griffin
Nigel Grimshaw

Contents

Communication   18
A personal letter   18
Self assessment   18

Step 1   8

Writing   9
Tell a story about yourself   9
Think out your content   9
Conversation with Mita   9
Write your own personal experience   11
Self assessment   11

Understanding   12
The talent   12
Find the facts   13

Oral work   14
The fisherman's tale   14
Discussion – can I make it up?   14

Spotlight on skills   15
Test yourself   15
The dictionary and thesaurus   15
Test yourself   15
Hearing new words   15
Reading new words   16
Games   16
Clues to words   16
Slang   16
Superlatives   16
The best word   17
Dictionary work – a word puzzle   17

Step 2   19

Writing   20
The kitchen (Arnold Wesker)   20
Write a short scene   23
Self assessment   23

Understanding   24
Holiday Island   24
Which word?   24
Definitions   24
Old people   25

Oral work   26
Discussion about jobs   26
Interviews   27

Spotlight on skills   28
Using a dictionary   28
Looking up a word   28
Spelling   29
Problem letters   29
Meanings   29
Stupid sentences   29

Communication   30
Young Person's Railcard   30
How to fill in a form   31

Step 3   32

Writing   33
Beginning a piece of writing   33
Judge and mark   35
Discussion   35
Self assessment   35

Understanding   36
Finding the exact details   36
Inflation (Dr Harold Priestley)   36

Oral work   38
'If I won a million pounds . . .'   38
Some things to think about   39
Some topics to discuss in small groups   39

Spotlight on skills   40
Write in sentences   40
Avoid over-using 'and'   41

Communication   41
Report on an athletic event   41
Athletic championships   41

Step 4   42

Writing   43
Describe a journey or a place – avoid cliché   43
Develop descriptive skills   44
The garden shed   45
Write your own description   46
Self assessment   46

Understanding   47
Choose and summarise   47
Tracks (John Hillaby)   47
Find the main facts   48
Summary   48
Choose and summarise for yourself   48
Factory fire (Leonard Rule)   49

Oral work   51
Using the telephone   51
Dial 999   51

Spotlight on skills   51
Punctuating speech 1   51
Points to watch   51
Write these out   52

Communication   52
Ordering the details   52
Making notes   52
Now make a note   53
Warning about notes   53
Notes for reports   54
Break-in   54

Step 5   56

Writing   57
A picture as a starting point   57
A story   57
Your reaction   58
Give your story a definite shape   58
Make sure your reaction has a pattern   58
Self assessment   58

Understanding   59
Picking out the points of an argument   59
Smoking   59
Find three reasons   59

Oral work   60
Discussion   60
Discussion in groups of four   60

Spotlight on skills   60
Speech punctuation 2   60

Communication   61
Business letters   61
Write a complete letter   63

Step 6   64

Writing   65
Hiroshima (John Hersey)   65
Building to a climax   67
Your own writing   68
Self assessment   68
Eye-witness account   69
Self assessment   69

Understanding   70
Multiple choice questions   70
Weather   70
The mugger   72
Questions on *The mugger*   73

Spotlight on skills   74
Using capitals   74

Communication   75
A letter of complaint   75
Answer a letter   75

Oral work   76
A telephone conversation   76

Step 7   77

Writing   78
The mill (Robert Westall)   78
Comparisons   80
A frightening experience   81
Write comments on Cathy's impressions   82
Find the comparisons   82
Write your own description   82
Self assessment   82

Understanding   83
Drawing your own conclusions   83
A wedding party in Spain (Laurie Lee)   83

Oral work   84
Chatting or giving a talk   85
Tape it   85
Prepare a talk   86
Begin your talk   87
The middle of the talk   88
End a talk   90
Some more ideas for talks   90

Spotlight on skills   91
More on capitals   91

Communication   92
Reporting   92
Was it a lion?   92
Making basic notes   93
Accident report   94
Write the report   94
Forest fire   95

Step 8   96

Writing   97
The raffle (V.S. Naipaul)   97
Write about Mr Hinds   101
Think again about Mr Hinds   101
Write your own description of a
person   101
Self assessment   101

Understanding   103
She's leaving home (the Beatles)   103

Oral work   104
Arrange a debate   104
Which is best?   105
Group work   105
Some ideas for debates   105
Proposing and seconding   106
Speaking in a debate   107

Spotlight on skills   107
Paragraphs   107

Communication   109
Write an article   109
Write a letter   109
Write a story   109
Self assessment   109

Step 9   110

Writing   111
A play to finish   111
Getting your own back   111
Write Scene 2 yourself   112
Self assessment   112

Understanding   113
Going home (Barry Hines)   113

Oral work   115
Work out your options   115
Role play – a meeting   115
Your point of view   117
Further role play   117

Spotlight on skills   118
The comma   118
Commas for lists   118
Commas in pairs   118

Communication   119
Make up your own advertisement   120

Step 10   121

Writing   122
Write about a family   122
Journey to Jo'burg (Beverley
Naidoo)   122
Self assessment   124

Understanding   125
View of a Pig (Ted Hughes)   125
The Irish Pig   125
Compare the poems – rhythm   126
Compare the poems – rhyme   126

Oral work   127
Raising money   127

Spotlight on skills   127
The apostrophe for omission   127
Problems with apostrophes   127

Communication   128
A choice of letters   128

Step 11   **129**

Writing   130
Look at the evidence   130
Last farewell to a contaminated island   130
Respond to a piece of writing   131
Self assessment   131

Understanding   132
In praise of volleyball   132
Judging points of view   132
Give your opinion   132
Bad behaviour by sports people   132

Oral work   133
Give your opinion   133

Spotlight on skills   134
The apostrophe for one person ownership   134

Communication   135
Write a memo   135

Step 12   **136**

Writing   137
Express a point of view   137
The changes I would like to see in my school   138
Comments on the writing   139
Self assessment   139

Understanding   140
The duck-walk (Keith Waterhouse)   140

Oral work   143
Changing customs   143

Spotlight on skills   144
Apostrophe to show more than one owner   144

Communication   144
Letters to annoy or letters to persuade   144
Which letter succeeds?   144
Write your own persuading letter   144

Step 13   **146**

Writing   147
A funny story   147
Counting the wrinkles (Betsy Byars)   147
Kes (Barry Hines)   148
Three men in a boat (Jerome K. Jerome)   149
A cheap repair   150
Write your own funny story   150
Self assessment   150

Understanding   151
Setting up camp (Cindy Buxton and Annie Price)   151

Oral work   154
Discuss racial bias and hooliganism   157

Spotlight on skills   157
Spelling – some advice   157

Communication   158
Directed writing – letter and report   158

Step 14   159

Writing   160
A frightening experience (Annette Tencha)   160
Write about your own childhood   161
Self assessment   161
Some final advice on writing   161

Understanding   162
Multiple choice   162
A fateful time (Vernon Scannell)   162
What you have to do   164

Oral work   166
The telephone   166

Spotlight on skills   167
Revision work   167
Self assessment   168

Communication   169
A council meeting   169
What you have to do   171
Write a letter – your point of view   171
A newspaper report favouring privatisation   172
What you have to do   172
A newspaper report opposing privatisation   173

Your coursework folio   174

Writing a story   174
Planning your folio   175
Different styles   175
Accuracy   175

List of authors   176
Extracts suitable for reading aloud   176

C

Throughout the book this symbol shows material suitable for coursework.

Step 1

In this Step you are shown how to:

■ prepare your ideas for writing about a personal experience.

You are asked to:

■ answer factual questions on *The talent*.

■ test whether you can make up a tale that sounds true.

■ find out how to impove your vocabulary.

■ write an interesting personal letter.

Writing

Tell a story about yourself

These titles are from different examination papers but they are all of the same type. They are asking you to tell a story about yourself. Examiners know that people write best about something that has happened to them.

1 *'Curiosity killed the cat but that didn't stop me.'*
   Write from personal experience about a time your need to find out brought you surprise or trouble.

2 *'I never felt so ashamed.'*
   Write about a personal experience – perhaps a joke that misfired or a time when you unthinkingly hurt someone – which ended with you feeling guilty or ashamed.

3 *'Losing a friend.'*
   Write about a time a friend moved to another district.

4 *'I've never felt so relieved in my life.'*
   Write from personal experience about a time something you dreaded never happened.

Think out your content

'I can't think of anything to write!' Most pupils have felt this at some time. Teachers hear it every day.

We will use the example of Mita to show how the problem might be overcome.

Mita remembers how her best friend, Deborah, went to live in Egypt for two years, but she can't think of how to write about her for two pages. We all need prompting to remember a story in detail. Read this conversation with Mita as if it were a play, two people taking the parts of Mita and her questioner.

Conversation with Mita

'Where did you first meet Deborah?'

'At primary school. Anyway she lived near me. Our mums put us together when we went in, so we sat together.'

'Did you help each other with work?'

5   'Well, she helped me mostly. She was good at maths, or numbers as we used to call it. I wasn't.'

'Did she mind helping you?'

'No – but she sometimes tried to get me into trouble. Like when she put all the wrong answers down, I copied them and then she altered hers

10   to the right ones when I wasn't looking. She only meant it as a joke – but I cried and hated her.'

'Did she get in trouble with teachers?'

'Well, not trouble, but she was cheeky. She said to Mrs Johnson, "I expect we'll be expecting a new teacher now you're expecting." Mrs

15   Johnson took it the wrong way – I suppose she thought it was cheeky because we were only about eight at the time.'

    'What did Deborah look like?'

    'Taller than me, but better looking I suppose. She had a round smiling face, blue eyes and fair hair. I think she looked so innocent. That's why
20   she was spoilt.'

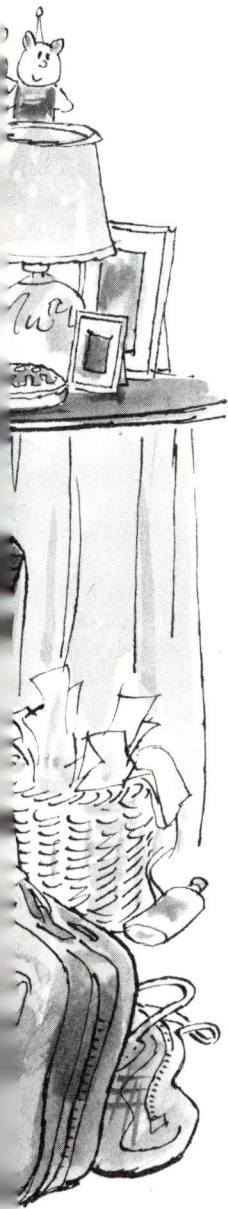

'Who spoilt her?'

'Everybody. The things she had for presents. Mind you I wasn't jealous, if that's what you're thinking. I was always round her house. She was generous. She gave me a watch once. She'd already got one.'

25 'Still got it?'

'Yes, but it doesn't work. I keep it though. I was going to throw it away, but when I heard she was going I decided I'd keep it.'

'When did you first hear she was going?'

'In our second year. We were thirteen then. We'd been friends for eight
30 years.'

'Did Deborah tell you she was going?'

'One day she just said, "I might be going to Egypt because my dad's going to work there." '

'How did you feel?'

35 'I didn't think anything of it at the time. I only half believed her. She was always exaggerating. Then it was definite. The funny thing was that at first I wondered who I would get to help me with maths. Then we started counting the days.'

'When was the last time you saw her?'

40 'The night before she left, round her house. Everything was all packed up. In fact we sat on a trunk and played *Fish, flower, fruit* – we used to play it a lot when we were younger.'

'Did you say much about leaving each other?'

'Not really. She kept saying she would possibly be back in a few
45 weeks. Her dad might not like it. But I didn't believe her. After a bit we couldn't think of much to say.'

'Did you give each other anything?'

'She'd brought me a calculator, a sort of joke because I couldn't do maths – but it was a good one. I've still got it. I gave her a necklace and
50 a brown paper bag, for her to be sick in. She was always sick travelling. She was sick all over our car once.'

'Did you write to each other?'

'For a bit. Then it got boring. She's back now. She lives at Marston.'

'So you see her?'

55 'Only once. Funny, we didn't really get on. I think she's more selfish and she's snobbish. Maybe it was going away, but perhaps we wouldn't have stayed friends anyway.'

Write your own personal experience

■ Before you write on one of the four topics, take it in turn to question your neighbour about what will be in it. The conversation might jog your memory about details that will help to make your writing sound convincing. You should write at least 300 words.

SELF ASSESSMENT

When you have written your experience change with a neighbour and decide whose sounds the most true.

Understanding

There will be different kinds of questions in the passages for understanding. The first type we look at is the question asking you to find the facts.

Read this passage.

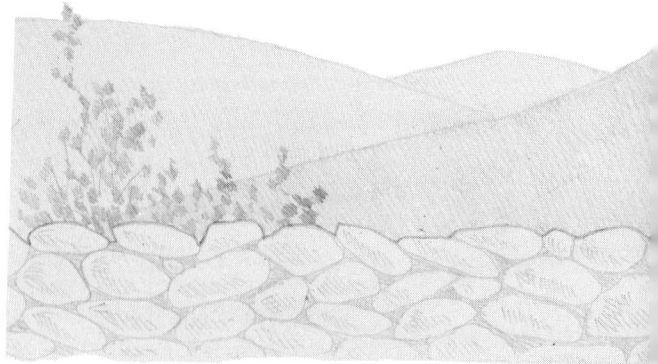

The talent

There were four of us in the party. We had been walking all day and we were tired. John, his wife Linda, and I had all been out walking together before. Steve, whom I knew only slightly, had asked to come along and I was regretting it. He had soon lagged behind. Time and again, before we
5   had even gone very far, he had stopped and we had had to wait for him to catch up. He had complained, too, partly about the hard going but mainly about the weather. For the past half hour, he had trudged along with us in gloomy silence.
   None of us had been exactly pleased about the weather. It had been
10 grey and misty all day. Now it was growing dark and the mist was getting thick. We couldn't see a light or a sign of life anywhere. We had just come to a track. John switched on his torch and we consulted the map. The track was marked on it. One way the track led back into wild country again. The other way took us to a farmhouse and then to a small village.
15 The problem was that we didn't know which way to take. John, who carried the compass, had lost it, probably when we stopped for lunch. There was no going back to look for it. We were lost and irritable.
   John thought we should go left up the track. Linda and I were for following it to the right. Steve stood a little way apart from us, saying
20 nothing.
   'Have it your way, then,' John grunted. 'We'll go right. But it'll take some time to find out if it's the wrong direction or not. If it is, then we'll have all that way to slog back.'
   Then Steve made us all jump. He barked, suddenly, like a dog. It was
25 an amazing imitation, loud and shrill. We gaped at him until we understood. Very faint and far away, came an answering bark. It could only have come from a dog at the farm and it came from down the track to our left. We set off that way.
   Steve gave that amazing bark once or twice more with the dog answering
30 until we could see the dim gleam of the farmhouse lights ahead.
   The dog, safely tied up, raged at us as we passed and shortly after that we were in the warmth and bustle of the village pub, sitting down to steak and kidney pie.

Find the facts

■ These questions are about facts, all of which you should find by looking back at the passage. Write your answers in complete sentences. Score 1 for each correct answer.

1 How many people were there in the walking party? (1)
2 What was the name of John's wife? (1)
3 How did the writer feel about having invited Steve to join them? (1)
4 What had the weather been like during the day? (1)
5 How did they manage to consult the map when it was dark? (1)
6 Why could they not line their map up with north and south? (1)

7 Who thought they should take the track to their left? (1)
8 How many people thought they should go to the right? (1)
9 What part did Steve take in the discussion? (1)
10 What did he suddenly do to startle the writer and the other two people? (1)
11 What answered him? (1)
12 How did that tell them which way they should take? (1)
13 What told them finally that they must be going the right way? (1)
14 Where did they eat that night? (1)

Oral work

The fisherman's tale

It's not much use telling you what happened last Thursday. You wouldn't believe it. I didn't believe it myself, till I actually put it on the scales. You know the bend in the river near Tyron's Mill? I sat there all day, next to old Alan Ryan. He got a shock, I can tell you. I'd caught a few perch and bream, nothing to shout about. It was three minutes to four that it happened. I know that because my watch stopped when it dragged me into the water. I've never played out line so fast in my life. Of course Alan was on hand to help. Took me a good hour to land him, but in the end he was in the net – a twenty-one pound sturgeon. No, I'm sorry you can't see him. Sent him to the British Museum. I've got a letter at home thanking me. They're going to have him stuffed.

Discussion – can I make it up?

The fisherman has tried to make his lie believable by filling it with detail that could be true – where he was fishing, the time, what he had caught before.

If you are among the many pupils who ask, 'Can I make it up?' before beginning a piece of writing, the answer is 'Yes', if you can make it sound real.

■ Prepare two stories to tell the class, one true and one false. Each should last about two minutes. Try to disguise your false story with real things. Be prepared to be questioned by the class for two minutes after you have finished your story. Remember you are only telling lies in the sense all good story-tellers do, making fiction (made-up stories) sound like fact.

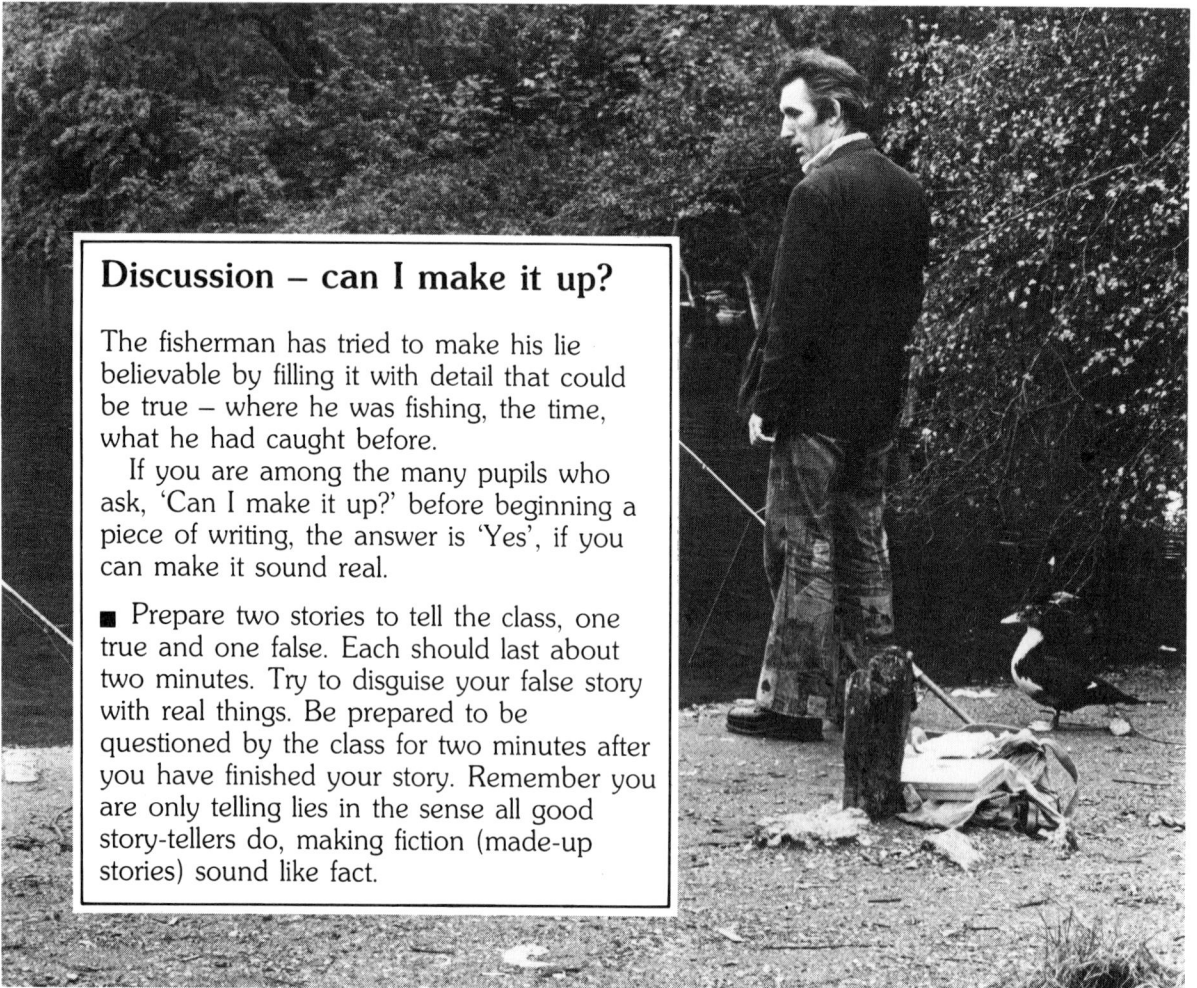

magpie

maid

majesty

magnolia

mainstream

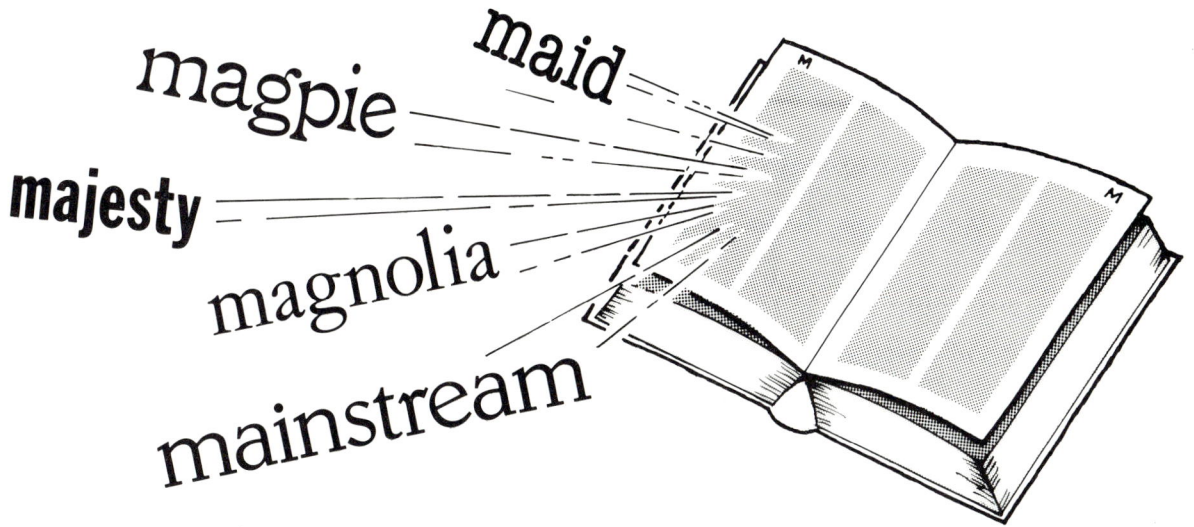

Spotlight on skills

☆ ☆ ☆ ☆ ☆ ☆ ☆ ☆ ☆ ☆ ☆ ☆

The more words you know the easier it is to express clearly what you mean.

Test yourself

A school dictionary normally contains between 30,000 and 40,000 words. How many do you know? Pick six pages for different letters at random. How many words do you really *know* on each page?

Find your average per page and multiply it by the number of the pages in the dictionary. If it is 11, 10, 9, 6, 12, 7, divided by six (pages) this will give you an average of 9 approximately. Multiply that 9 by the number of pages in the dictionary and you will have a rough idea of how many words you know.

The dictionary and thesaurus

In your fifth year at school always have a dictionary and thesaurus close by. A thesaurus lists words under headings, eg:

433 Yellowness – N yellowness, canary yellow; yellow metal, gold, crocus, buttercup, primrose, daffodil, saffron, mustard; topaz; lemon, honey, biliousness, jaundice . . .

■ Use four of the words for *yellowness* in separate sentences. Use them as describing words – adjectives.

A thesaurus will remind you of words you know but may not have thought of using. It will also give you new words.

To use your dictionary and thesaurus properly make sure you know the alphabet well.

Test yourself

■ Put these words in the order they come in a dictionary:

main   maintain   maid   magpie   magnolia maintenance   mainstream   majesty majority   mainly   mail

Hearing new words

If you hear a new word, look it up. If you cannot find it, your teacher will help you. Then try using it.

Reading new words

Never let a new word pass by you that you do not understand. Look it up at once in a dictionary. If the meaning is still not clear, ask your teacher. *Immediately* write a sentence using it.

Games

Play word games like *Scrabble*.
Do simple newspaper and magazine crosswords.
Do word puzzles in magazines.

Clues to words

Prefixes often give clues to the meaning of a word. Look at the meanings of these prefixes:

Prefix	Meaning	Example
ab, abs	away from	absent
ambi	both	ambidextrous
ante	before	antenatal
anti	opposite	anti-aircraft
bi	two	biplane
bio	life	biography
circum	around	circumference
contra	against	contradict
omni	all	omnivore
poly	many	polytechnic
post	after	postscript
pre	before	prenatal
re	again	rewrite
semi	half	semi-detached
tele	far	telephone
trans	across	transatlantic
tri	three	triangle

■ Pick any ten of these prefixes and make a list of words you find in the dictionary beginning with them. Look at the meanings.
■ Test a friend on the meanings of ten prefixes.

Slang

■ Do not use slang in writing unless you are using actual conversation in a story or play. Remove this slang. Discuss first, then rewrite.

1 He bashed him in the gob.
2 She's got a lot of bottle.
3 The boy was nicked for pinching a bike.
4 The girl bunked off from school and got it in the neck.

Superlatives

■ Do not use common superlatives in writing unless you are using actual conversation in a play or a story. Replace the underlined superlatives by using words that make the meaning more precise:

1 We had a really great time.
2 It was a smashing party.
3 The new record was really ace.
4 I thought the blouse was brill.

smashing Brill ACE great

The best word

■ It is always best to use the word that fits or describes closely what you want to say. In this exercise you are given three words to choose from. Picture a dirty boy and an unused canal. Copy out the passage, choosing the best word. **Do not mark this book.**

The { untidy / scruffy / unclean } boy { raced / rode / pedalled } his { dilapidated / rusty / neglected } bike down to the

{ disused / old / shut } canal. He { strained / struggled / puffed } to ride over the { hump-backed / steep / arched } bridge

and then { free-wheeled / descended / came down } onto the pot-holed towpath. The water in

the canal was { stagnant / weed-filled. / putrid } No boats had { sailed / been / plied } on there for years.

No { darting / silver-scaled / glinting } fish tempted the angler to its { rubbishy / despoiled / litter-strewn } banks.

Dictionary work – a word puzzle

The answers start with pat.
1 Which *pat* might you have on your jeans? (patch)
2 Which *pat* might you eat?
3 Which *pat* do you take out for an invention?
4 Which *pat* means fatherhood?
5 Which *pat* goes ahead of a group?
6 Which *pat* is to do with disease?
7 Which *pat* means to control yourself?
8 Which *pat* is in hospital?
9 Which *pat* is a friendship?
10 Which *pat* is a bishop?
11 Which *pat* defends his or her country?
12 Which *pat* means to act as if you are better or more important?

Make a habit of looking at your dictionary often. It can make very interesting reading. This dictionary habit can help you to understand what words mean and improve your spelling.

Communication

A personal letter

If you were writing to thank your Gran for a present, you could write:

Dear Gran
Thank you for the trainers
you sent for my birthday.
They were very nice.
Love
Jane

Your Gran would be pleased that you had taken the trouble to write to thank her, but she would be disappointed in the lack of news in the letter.

Think: How you like to receive long letters.
Ask yourself: What would the person like to know about me?

■ Write a letter to a relation in which you include these things. Write in sentences. Make each of these topics a short paragraph:

1 The present and how you like it. Perhaps what you plan to do with it.
2 What you did on your birthday.
3 Some of the other presents you received, particularly clothes.

4 Any news of your family and pets.
5 How school is going.
6 What you are planning to do in the next few weeks.
7 Anything of interest that has happened to neighbours the relation knows.
8 When you hope next to see them.

SELF ASSESSMENT

When you have written your letter change with a neighbour and decide which would be the most interesting to receive through the post.

Step 2

In this Step you are shown how to:

■ read a play, *The Kitchen* and add a scene.

You are asked to:

■ answer questions that test your knowledge of the meaning of words in two passages, *Holiday island* and *Old people.*

■ take part in interviews to discover which type of job suits you.

■ improve your dictionary skills.

■ apply for a Young Person's Railcard and a driving licence.

Writing

The Kitchen

Lights fade up on the sound of a guitar.
It is afternoon break. **Paul** and **Raymond** are working in their corner. These are the only two who stay through the afternoon. **Kevin** is flat out on his back on a wooden bench, exhausted. **Dimitri** is slowly sweeping up. **Peter** is sitting by a table waiting for Monique. **Hans** is in a corner with a guitar, singing *Ah Sinner-man* in German.

Kevin	Finished! I'm done! I'm boiled! You can serve me up for supper.
Paul	(*As if ordering a meal*). Two portions of boiled Irishman please! With garnish!
Raymond	(*also calling*) Two fried tomatoes on his ears, potatoes round his head, and stuff his mouth with an extra helping of peas.
Kevin	I'll produce me own gravy! But did you see it? Did you see that? Fifteen hundred customers, and half of them eating fish. I had to start work on a Friday!
Raymond	It's every day the same, my friend.
Kevin	(*raising himself up*) Look at me. I'm soaking. Look at this jacket. I can wring it out. That's not sweat, no man carries that much water. (*flopping back again*) Kevin, you'll drop dead if you stay. I'm warning you, Kevin, take a tip from a friend, hop it! Get out! You've got your youth Kevin, keep it! This is no place for a human being – you'll drop dead, I'm telling you.
Dimitri	Hey Irishman, what you grumbling about this place for? Is different anywhere else? People come and people go, big excitement, big noise. (*makes noise and gesticulates*) What for? In the end who do you know? You make a friend, you going to be all you life his friend but when you go from here – pshtt! You forget! Why you grumble about this one kitchen?
Peter	You're a very intelligent boy, Dimitri.
Dimitri	And you're a bloody fool. I'm not sure I want to talk with you.
Kevin	Oh not the Gaston row again. All the morning I hear how Peter gave Gaston a black eye. It's the break, no rows please, it's peace. Can you hear it? It's lovely, it's silence. It's nothing – ahhh! (*moves*) Oooh – I'm drowning, in my own sweat. Christ! What a way to die.
Dimitri	(*to Peter*) A bloody fool you!

Write a short scene

■ Write a short scene from a play, setting it out as this playwright has done in *The Kitchen*. Put in both speech and stage directions. The scene of your play is a school. The time is just after the bell has gone for the end of the day. Three characters are waiting to see a female teacher. She is late. They hang around and dicuss the day, homework and what she wants to see them about. Give each some characterization, for example, one will not help with homework; one is a bully; one is afraid, etc. You could end up with them playing about like they did in *The Kitchen*.

SELF ASSESSMENT

When you have written your scene divide into groups of four, read each scene and decide which character you would most like to act.

Understanding

Some questions test your understanding of a passage by examining your knowledge of the words in it and the way they are used. Read this and then look at the questions.

● ●

Holiday island

Lakos is a delightful island, fertile and green, with plenty of rolling country to explore. The north-west part is covered by low-lying mountains but the southern part is well-populated and the main area for farming and manufacturing.

There is a wide choice of shelving sandy beaches and swimming in the warm sea is generally safe but for those who enjoy more active pursuits there are opportunities for wind-surfing, para-gliding and sailing in the main town of Toros.

● ●

Which word?

■ If you answer the question in the form of a sentence, do not forget to put quotation marks round the word that has been asked for, like this: 'delightful'. Score 1 for each answer.

1 Which word in the passage suggests that the land on the island consists of shallow valleys and low hills? (1)
2 Which word indicates that the mountains are not very high? (1)
3 Which word tells you that quite a lot of people live in the south-western part of the island? (1)
4 Which word indicates that the beaches do not dip very steeply into the sea? (1)
5 Which word could be replaced by the phrase 'ways of spending one's leisure time'? (1)

Definitions

You may have used a dictionary to help you with some of the last questions or to check that you were right. You may need a dictionary for the following exercise. This is a harder kind of question. You are not asked to pick out a word but to say what a word means.

To be successful at this kind of question, two things are needed. You need a wide vocabulary so that you have a very good chance of having come across the word several times before. You also need to have had practice at explaining the meaning of words, either by another word meaning the same, which is called a synonym, or in a phrase, which is a few words.

■ You are given a word or a phrase from the passage and asked to explain what it means. Read the following and do the questions which follow it. Score 2 for a good definition.

Old people

Old people seem to remember their youth as better than it really was. The summers of their past seem to have been hotter and more full of sunshine than our summers today. They recall a past tranquillity, a pace of life that was slower and more comfortable. This is not to say that they knowingly exaggerate. When talking to some old people, though, one senses that their memories, coloured by nostalgia, sometimes deceive them.

■ Explain in your own words the meaning of:

1 tranquillity (2)
2 pace (2)
3 exaggerate (2)
4 coloured by nostalgia (2)

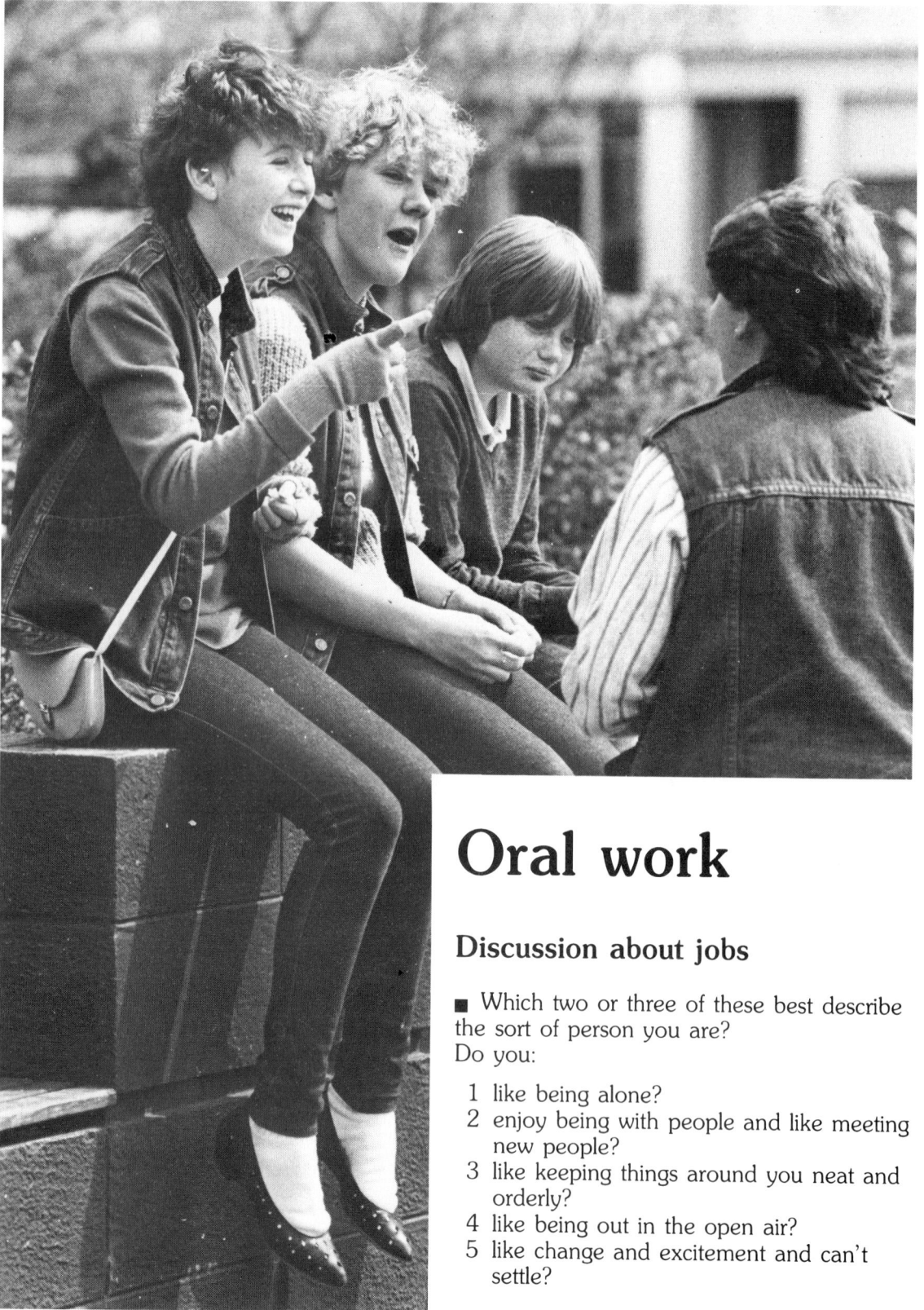

Oral work

Discussion about jobs

■ Which two or three of these best describe the sort of person you are?
Do you:

1 like being alone?
2 enjoy being with people and like meeting new people?
3 like keeping things around you neat and orderly?
4 like being out in the open air?
5 like change and excitement and can't settle?

6 like looking after other people and feeling wanted?
7 prefer animals to human beings?
8 dislike being ordered about?
9 like travel and going to places you have never seen before?
10 like familiar places and dislike the new and unknown?
11 like power and being in control of things or people?
12 enjoy working with figures and things mathematical?
13 enjoy looking smart and wearing smart clothes?
14 enjoy sport and outdoor activities?

■ Discuss, as a class or as a group, which of these qualities listed would make you fit into which of these jobs.

shop assistant   swimming pool attendant
hairdresser's assistant   building site worker
delivering leaflets from door to door
window cleaning   working in a café
working in a pet shop   working at a horse
riding stables   working in an office
working in a nursery for small children
bank clerk   police   motor-cycle messenger

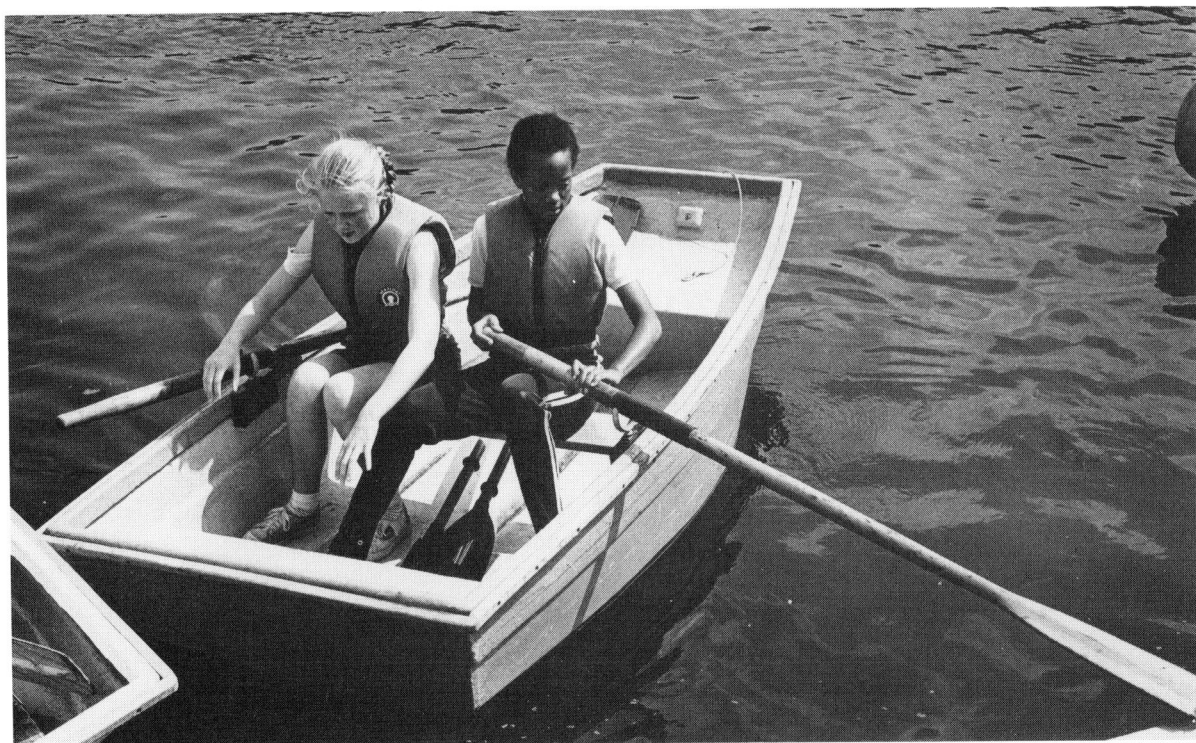

Interviews

■ Four or five people form the interviewing team. Members of the class apply and are interviewed for the job they think will suit them. The team, after interviewing, either take them on or decide they are unsuitable.
The class might then discuss how good at its job the interviewing team has been.

```
A B C D E F G H I J K L M
a b c d e f g h i j k l m
N O P Q R S T U V W X Y Z
n o p q r s t u v w x y z
```

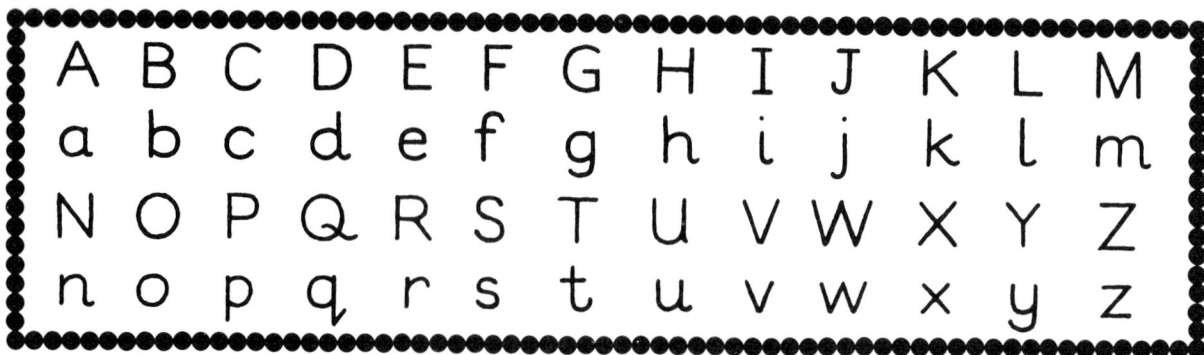

Spotlight on skills

☆ ☆ ☆ ☆ ☆ ☆ ☆ ☆ ☆ ☆ ☆

Using a dictionary

You won't be able to use a dictionary unless you know the alphabet.

■ How quickly can you do these exercises and get them all right?

1 How many letters are out of order in the list? The quickest way may be to write out the alphabet, checking against this list.
a b c d f e g h i j l k m n o p r q s t u v w x y z

2 How many letters are out of order in this list?
a b c d e f h g i j k l m n o p q s r t v u w x y z

3 Complete this part of the alphabet up to **p**.
i j k . . .

4 Complete this up to **v**.
p q . . .

5 Complete this up to **j**.
d . . .

If you couldn't do all the exercises quickly and without mistakes, you need to learn the alphabet so that you can repeat it without thinking.

Looking up a word

■ Start with the first letter of a word to look it up in a dictionary. Some dictionaries give several words in their definitions. Write down the first definition you find of these words.

pensive   feline   notion   wistful   gesture vulgar

■ If you are looking up words which begin with the same letter, look at the second letter to find where the word comes in the dictionary. **R**o**ad** comes after **r**e**ad** since **o** comes after **e** in the alphabet. Put these words into dictionary order.

pin   pun   pen   pot   pan

Now check in the dictionary to see that you got them right.

■ If you are looking up words which begin with the same two letters, you look at the third letter to find where the word comes in the dictionary. **Fad** comes before **fang**, because **d** comes before **n** in the alphabet. Put these words into dictionary order.

proud   preen   pram   prince   prune

Check your answer with a dictionary.

■ No matter how many letters – two, three, four or five – are the same at the beginning of a word, **look at the first letter that is different.** Then use alphabetical order to find the order of the words in a dictionary. Put these into dictionary order.

dictionary   dictate   diction   dictator dictatorship
Check with your dictionary.

Spelling

One use of a dictionary is to check spelling. Correct the mis-spellings in this list.

altogether   about   begining   beleive disappear   easily   early   everbody February   freind   famly   happen   hight idea   imposible   jealous   langage   lissened medicine   necessary   neibour   occasionally plesant   rember   shinning   sincerely something   tempry   tough   usually   wierd

How many were wrong?

Problem letters

■ Words, as you know, may not be spelled as they are spoken. Here is a guide list of beginning letters:

c can be <u>k</u> (kitchen) or <u>s</u> (services)
f can be <u>ph</u> (photograph)
gu can be spoken with a silent <u>u</u> as in (guard) or as <u>gw</u> (guano)
h the <u>high</u> sound can be <u>hy</u> as well as <u>hi</u>
n can be <u>kn</u> (knuckle) or <u>pn</u> (pneumonia)
qu is usually spoken as <u>k</u>
s can be <u>c</u> (ceiling) or <u>ps</u> (psychology)
w can be <u>r</u> (write)

Meanings

■ One word may have several different meanings. Give as many different meanings as you can find for the following words. We used a good dictionary and put the score against each word.

1 bay (five meanings)
2 boom (two meanings)
3 bush (two meanings)
4 dock (four meanings)
5 hamper (two meanings)
6 punch (three meanings)

Stupid sentences

■ One word in each of the following sentences makes it sound ridiculous. What is the word and what does it mean? (Use a dictionary.)

1 He played the clavicle beautifully.
2 Roaring and showing its fangs, the yaffle chased them across the ice.
3 He enjoyed the well-cooked termagant and potatoes.
4 She wore a fashionable caisson.
5 He took his refectory a walk on its lead.

The pamphlet

Do you qualify for a Young Persons Railcard?
Yes if you are
a) 16 and under 24 years of age at the time of purchase.
Or
b) A student of any age who is in full time education attending an education establishment for over 15 hours weekly for at least 20 weeks a year.

How to get your Railcard
Get two copies of a passport-style photo of yourself.
Fill in the application form.
You need to take proof that you're:
a) under 24 (your birth certificate or passport)
Or
b) a student (the application form and one of the photos must be signed by your headmaster/tutor/head of department).
NB. If you're a student buying your Railcard at your College/Campus Student travel office then your College Registration Card bearing your photograph is all you need to show.
Take the application form, your photographs and £12 to any principal British Rail station, Appointed Travel Agent or authorised Student Travel office.

Ask about the Inter Rail card which costs about £120 and offers one month's free Second Class travel on most railways in Western Europe, Scandinavia and Morocco.

Where your Railcard doesn't give you a discount
1. London Underground Trains, Glasgow PTE Underground Trains, Tyne and Wear Metro Trains, and most other trains not run by British Rail.
2. Special Excursions (i.e. not listed in public timetables).
3. Nightrider trains, Railair Coach Links.
4. "Boat Trains" between London (Victoria) and Dover, Folkestone and Newhaven, London (Waterloo) and Southampton. (You can travel on all the other trains between these places.)
5. On Friday's you cannot go on trains timed to leave from London King's Cross between 1355 hrs and 1903 hrs inclusive.

Conditions
1. You must sign your Railcard.
2. Your Railcard is not transferable to anyone else nor are the tickets bought with it. The Railcard remains, at all times, British Railways Board property.
3. When asked by British Rail staff, please show your Railcard and ticket, otherwise the full fare will be payable as if you had no Railcard.
4. If the Railcard gets defaced, illegible, or torn, it will not be valid. You can get a replacement, but you'll have to pay a fee.
5. The Board may refuse to issue or renew a Railcard. It won't undertake to replace lost or stolen Railcards.

We're getting there

Communication

Young Person's Railcard

■ Study this pamphlet. Then your teacher will either give you a copy of the form or ask you to copy it from this book.
Do not mark this book in any way.

1 How much does a Young Person's Railcard cost?
2 Who can obtain a Young Person's Railcard?
3 What can you do for £120?
4 What do you need besides the completed form and the money to obtain a railcard?
5 Name two underground railways you cannot travel on.
6 What trains can't you travel on from King's Cross?
7 What is the stipulation about boat trains?
8 Can a brother or sister use the same card?
9 What must you do if the card gets damaged?
10 What does: 'Don't forget that both Railcard and ticket must be current when travelling' mean?

■ Now complete the form. It needs the signature of a teacher. He or she will tell you what to do about this.

How to fill in a form

■ Your teacher will give you an Application for Your Driving Licence.

1 **Read** all the **instructions** and look at the form before you write anything at all.
2 Fill in first in **pencil** so you can easily cross out or rub out mistakes.
3 Use black ink if asked for.
4 Some parts of the form may require **block letters**: for example, A B C, not a b c.
5 Learn your birth year, your postcode and your National Insurance Number.

■ Now fill in the copy of this form your teacher will give you.

■ Fill it in first as if applying for a licence for the first time. Then add the details as if you had lost your licence.

Step 3

In this Step you are shown how to:

- make judgements on the beginnings of five pupils' work.

You are asked to:

- discuss your judgements and begin a piece of your own.
- find the exact details in an article on Inflation.
- continue a discussion in role.
- make a report on an athletic event.

Writing

Beginning a piece of writing

■ These are opening paragraphs on the subject **Pets are never easy to train**. Read them and answer the questions that follow.

A

Mrs Jones was determined to train Ben to be an obediant and loyal dog. He was two years old and she knew it was going to be a difficult job.

She had rescued Ben from the local dogs home three days earlier. He had been there for two months, ever since he had been found roaming a nearby town. Mrs Jones had been told that Ben was about to be shot because an owner had not been found for him. She immediately took pity on the large, rather ugly dog and took him home with her that day.

Anne (15)

B

Some pets are easy to train, others need alot of time spent with them and affection and love to make them feel safe and assured. All pets can be trained to do things even if it's just where their toilet and food dishes are. It takes alot of time and patience to train pets, especally dogs, which probably need the most training out of all pets.

Ben (15)

C

'A man's best friend is a dog' – or so they say. We once owned a dog, though, that, although very good-natured, could never be trained.

I remember first seeing it – a small, black, bundle of smooth, silky fur, huddled in the corner of an 'R.S.P.C.A. dog shelter' kennel. The kennel assistant tied a piece of rope around the dog's neck and brought him out. He sidled up to me, blinking stupidly in the bright light. His tail was tucked right between his legs – almost touching his stomach. After a while, though, the tail slowly dropped and the tip began to wag.

Verinder (15)

D

'Sit!', I commanded. 'Sit! Goldie! Sit! On, for heafen's sake!'
Goldie stood gazing at me, tongue lolling out and tail wagging. I bent
down and stroked his head.
'Look stupid, when I say "Sit", you sit.'
I stood up again 'Sit Goldie!' Goldie lay down.
'Tut, oh well, I suppose it's a start.'

Goldie was a Golden Labrador and belonged to my Aunt, and I was
helping her to train him. Goldie Labrador's are *supposed* to be renowned
for their intelligence, but not Goldie!

John (15)

E

Many people nowadays have pets of some sort, though it is probably
dogs that require the most training of all animals in the home. When
people by a dog they never realise whats coming. They see that all of
their friends have one so they think they would like one too. This is when
the problem comes. A dog that is truely loved and wanted is bought and
taken home to a household that does'nt know how to look after dogs.
The pet will be given a great amount of attention though this soon
vanishes when the pet starts to behave dangerously.

Pets, like hamsters can be trained by just handeling them each day when
their young to give them confidence in you. When you've bought one
and have'nt got time to play with it it may bight you because it's afraid of
you. This isn't just not very nice for you but it's very cruel on the
hamster.

Gail (16)

Judge and mark

1 List the starts in order of interest, starting with the most interesting and ending with the least. (Judge interest by deciding which start makes you most want to read on.)
2 Which writer is going to make up a story? What signs are there that the story so far has been made up?
3 Which two are definitely going to be about personal experience of training a pet?
4 Which two are general statements about training pets?
5 List the spelling and punctuation mistakes in each one.
6 Which start shows the best variety in use of words and punctuation marks?
7 Give a mark out of 10 for each piece.

Discussion

■ Compare your answers and decide:
Is there any connection between the type of start and the interest?
Do the paragraphs that are written about personal experience of training seem more interesting than those which make general statements?
Is the interest connected with accuracy?
Does a large number of spelling mistakes affect your attitude to what is written?
Is conversation a good way to start a piece of writing?

■ Now write your own opening paragraphs on **Pets are never easy to train** or **A man's best friend is a dog.**

SELF ASSESSMENT

Divide into groups of four. Decide who has written the most interesting opening.

Understanding

Finding the exact details

■ Certain kinds of questions ask you to give exact details, like numbers and dates, from a passage. Read the passage carefully but do not try to remember all the details. Then read the questions.

You may need to use some of your own words in each answer. The information should be exact. This will mean that you have to copy details from the passage.

Inflation

The twentieth century has seen more changes than any other in the amount of goods that the pound sterling can buy. There was a time when a working class family could buy all their weekly groceries for less than £1, when the wages of the working person were less than £2, his or her rent not more than five to six shillings a week (25 to 30 new pence), and a joint of beef costing £1.25 a pound today could be bought for ten old pence (4 new pence).

Wages, like prices, were, at the beginning of the period with which we are dealing here (1851) a mere fraction of what they are now. There was no state retirement pension nor any general government pension scheme, no unemployment or state sickness benefit. The destitute were taken to the workhouses or paid small sums of a few shillings a week by the Parish Overseers of the Poor.

On the other hand, life was much more simple. There was none of the articles which are now considered almost necessities by the average householder – the car, the vacuum cleaner, the refrigerator, the deep freeze, the washing machine, the radio, stereo, television set and many of the household gadgets we see advertised.

Although there were rises in prices during war years (1914–1918 and 1939–1945), rapid inflation did not come into Great Britain until after the Second World War, reaching its alarming climax in 1977. By that time the general public had become increasingly alarmed by the rising costs which had only partly been met by wage rises. The Government, trade unions and employers tried to achieve some kind of wage parity by limited rises in pay and by control of prices. At that time the goal of the Government was single figure inflation, that is, less than ten pence in the pound every year.

adapted from *The What It Cost the Day Before Yesterday Book* by Dr Harold Priestley

1 When a working person's wages were £2 a week, what was his or her probable rent – in new pence? (1)

2 What date marks the beginning of the period dealt with in the passage? (1)

3 What kind of employment benefit was paid at that time? (2)

4 What happened to the poor and destitute in those days? (1)

5 What articles did not exist at that time for the average householder? Name three of them. (3)

6 Give the dates for the beginning and end of the two world wars that have happened in this century. (2)

7 In what year does the passage say that inflation reached its climax in this country? (1)

8 How does the passage define 'single figure inflation'? (2)

Oh boy! *Gimme another!*

MALTESERS

CHOCOLATE COATED MALTED MILK

THE ENERGY CHOCOLATES

Simply BAGS of nourishment!

Pop one in, pop two in . . . three . . . you won't be able to resist these little chocolate bubbles, smooth outside and crunchy in ! Maltesers are made of crisped-up malted milk coated in cream-smooth milk chocolate. De- licious they are, and good for you, ready packed in handy bags to munch at the pictures or at home. Get some tonight !

2d MADE BY *Mars*

Made LIGHT to be digestible — non-fattening.

There's real Malted Milk in the crisp centres of Maltesers—that means *food value* added to the nourishment of the milk chocolate coat- ing ; at the same time they are made light and crunchy by specially-invented machines, ex- pressly to be easily digestible and absolutely *non-fattening.*

Oral work

Here is a transcript of a discussion by five young people.

'If I won a million pounds . . .'

J. If I won a million pounds, I'd buy a new house for my Mum and Dad instead of the <u>grotty</u> flat we live in. It'd be in the country with a swimming pool and . . .

T. I wouldn't give any money to <u>me</u> parents. I mean what do parents do for you? I'd go round the world. Have a great time.

N. That's selfish!

T. I won the money, didn't I? What's selfish about that?

N. <u>Yeh</u>, but your Mum brought you up.

T. <u>Me</u> Mum <u>dragged me up</u>.

O. You'd have a job er. . . spending, er. . . a million, er. . . I mean . . . um. . . that's, er. . . a lot of money, er. . .

T. Not me, <u>mate</u>, I'd find plenty to do with it. Just think, you would never have to work again. You could live in luxury. Live in the South of France or some tropical Caribbean island.

O. Yes, er. . . but that's not good, er. . . for you. You need to, um. . . do something. . . to keep your, er. . . mind occupied.

N. I would give some away.

T. More fool you. Nobody ever give <u>me nothing</u>.

J. The first thing I'd do is to go to a <u>posh</u> hotel for a meal. I'd take my Gran. She's always wanted to go to a <u>posh</u> hotel.

N. That's just wasting it.

J. Why? Giving an old person a treat?

N. There are people in the world who really need food to survive.

T. Hark at goodie, goodie. I bet you'd spend it on yourself!

N. I wouldn't.

R. Surely, if you won a million pounds, there is scope for helping both yourself and other people. The first thing to do would be to invest the money so that it brings in a good income. This country needs investment, too. Then you could decide how best to use the income to help both yourself and others. Meanwhile you would still have a million pounds.

1. Continue the discussion in groups of four or five.
    or
2. In the same groups take on the roles of J.N.T.O. and R. Argue as you think they might.

Some things to think about

Should the one who says the most get the most marks?
Should the most aggressive speaker get most marks?
Should the most sensible speaker get the most marks?
Should the one you think pleases the teacher get most marks?
Should O lose marks for his or her 'ums' and 'ers'?
Should you lose marks if you interrupt?
Should the one who says least get least marks?
Should you lose marks for bad grammar and slang (underlined in the transcript)?

■ Now mark J.N.T.O. and R out of 10 for their contribution to the discussion.

Some topics to discuss in small groups

1 What is the best thing ever invented?
2 How I will cast my vote when I am eighteen and why.
3 All animals, including circus animals, should be fully protected.
4 You can't believe in ghosts nowadays.
5 The world I would like to help make.
6 Nobody should be able to pay for hospital treatment. It should be done on the National Health in strict turn.
7 It's really a man's world. Women are second class citizens.

39

Spotlight on skills

☆ ☆ ☆ ☆ ☆ ☆ ☆ ☆ ☆ ☆ ☆

Write in sentences

Many candidates lose marks for not writing in sentences. Will you? This often happens when you are asked to write a number of words. You count the words, but forget about the sentences. Much can be written about the English sentence. Your main task is to be able to spot when you have written one. Remember – a comma can never do the job of a full-stop.

■ Where are the full-stops (including one question mark) missing here?

Sara was sure she had seen the picture somewhere before it rang a bell in her mind the old man with the moustache reminded her of something had she not walked down that road once something dimly stirred in her memory and she became excited

■ Many candidates do not punctuate the short sentence. You should find six here:

He jumped the stream his feet missed the stone he slipped now he was deep in mud thunder rolled above him it was a dreadful day

■ Look at this sentence:

I saw a strange box in the field where the old oak stands.

How many sentences are there in it? Can you spot three?

I saw a strange box.
I saw a strange box in the field.
I saw a strange box in the field where the old oak stands.

But you could not punctuate it:

I saw a strange box. In the field. Where the old oak stands.

The second is a phrase and the third is a clause. They do not make sense on their own and, therefore, they can not stand as sentences. They are part of a longer sentence. Remember – a sentence must make sense.

■ How many sentences can you find in these?

1 The roof was falling in over the doctor's flat.

2 The horse was tired and limping.

3 I caught a mole in its tunnel by the hawthorn bush.

4 The record was the best to be played during the whole week by the disc-jockey.

5 The evidence against him was put by the judge in a very clear manner.

6 The weather was extremely hot and close while the championships were held and six people fainted.

Avoid over-using 'and'

As a rough rule you can say that just one 'and' to a sentence is enough. Do not put too many 'ands' in any piece of writing. Do not begin with 'and'.

■ Rewrite this piece. Use no more than two 'ands':

It was hot in the street and I was sweating and this ice-cream van came round the corner and crashed into a wall and the side of the van ripped open and out came boxes of ice-creams and the kids rushed up and opened them and the driver who was not hurt could not stop them.

Communication

C

Reporting on an athletic event

In summarising and sometimes in reporting, you need to pick out the important facts from detail. Read the following:

Athletic championships

The Wessex Intermediate Girls' County Championships were held at Duncton Stadium on Saturday. Despite a high wind and rain there were some good performances. The outstanding event was a long jump of 5 metres 41 cm by Jane Akabuti. This beat the existing record by 3 cm. It was achieved in her last jump when she was lying second to Rachel Abrahams. The 1500 metres was a close tussle between Judy Hitchcock and Maureen Feldman, which Judy took by half a metre. Kate Lane won the 100 metres, but her fast time of 12.5 seconds was not ratified because of a following wind. A name to look for in the future is Tina Norford, who although only 15, won the 400 metres.

■ Now answer these questions in as few words as you can:
What were the championships?
Where were they held?
What was the outstanding event?
Who won the 1500 metres?
Name two other winners.

■ Now write a short report of not more than 40 words on the Athletic Championships. Use your short answers to the above questions. Write each one out in the form of a sentence, putting the sentences into an order that seems most sensible to you.

Step 4

In this Step you are shown how to:

■ avoid stale ideas (clichés).

■ judge a description and write about a favourite sport.

■ make a summary.

You are asked to:

■ practise using the telephone.

■ develop your use of speech punctuation.

■ make notes in preparation for a report on a *Break-in*.

Writing

Describe a journey or a place – avoid cliché

Read these three openings to descriptions of **A journey from the town to the countryside**.

A

The train jolted and began moving slowly through the vast junction of King's Cross station. The crackly tannoy system, the cries of the porters and the buzz of the tightly-packed station faded away to be replaced by the more soothing regular noise of the train picking up speed.

Out of the window I saw the drab backs of seedy warehouses, the grimy sides of goods wagons and stacks of rotting wood.

An old man paused and stared at the train, waiting for it to pass before he continued picking his way across the lattice-work of tracks, clutching an armful of timber.

This was the face of North London, drab and grey, giving an impression of loneliness.

Janice (16)

B

The first thing you noticed as you left the town and entered the country was the change in the colour of the sky. The sky in the town was grey and full of smog. The country had a crystal blue sky.

The houses were also different. The town's houses were like broken glass on a wall with completely different peaks all clustered together. The country's houses were spaced out and picturesque.

The people we saw in the country were different too. They were plump, jolly and red-faced, while the ones we were used to in the town were tall, lean and serious.

The town noises were loud noises, car engines and construction machines all joined together. In the country we could hear birds singing and sheep bleating.

Kay (15)

C

We could see the crumbling limestone cliff we were heading for as we rode into Buxton. Over the cliff top into the next valley is a narrow road through peaceful countryside. But the only way to the countryside is the road through the centre of the town.

Alan rode ahead. He wanted to show off his skill at weaving through the traffic, but I caught him at the lights.

'What's your hurry? I shouted, but I don't think he heard. The cars behind and at the side of us were revving and inching forward trying to anticipate the lights.

The man in a huge silver car next to me was lighting a cigarette. As the lights turned yellow he started to draw away, his hand off the wheel. I edged nearer the pavement. The town is a dangerous place for cyclists.

Tom (16)

■ Read these comments and decide which of the pieces each one best fits.

1 Certainly written about a remembered journey.
2 Completely made-up.
3 Gives a good impression of a dirty town.
4 Contains details that are simply not true any more.
5 Tells you something about the writer as well as what he or she is describing.
6 Shows the best sentence structure and vocabulary.
7 Full of **clichés** – ideas and expressions that are so common they make no impact on your imagination.
8 Makes a comment on a town other than the usual ones about dirt and noise.

■ Use the answers to the questions as the basis for a five-line comment on each piece.

Develop descriptive skills

Many pieces of description are like passage B, having no thought or purpose, simply a list of cliché thoughts and expressions. In a description of a place, scene or journey you should write about your own feelings. The reader must know how the writer feels or he will not be interested. Descriptions are best written from remembered experience.

■ Read this description of a garden shed

The garden shed

Last Saturday I went to the bottom of our garden to fetch the sunbed
from our shed. I twisted the wooden latch and stepped carefully inside.
The first obstacle was the handles of the lawnmower. I edged round them,
careful not to touch the shelf above the window. One false move and I
5   would be crowned by anything from my sister's roller-skates to a tin of
nails. The old floor boards creaked as I shuffled across the floor looking
for a piece of sunbed sticking out from under a pile. I decided it might be
under the rubber dinghy. It wasn't. But it might be under the mattress
that was under the dinghy. I stood on the dinghy because there was
10   nowhere to put it and pulled carefully on the mattress, ready to scream if
a mouse rushed out. The mattress was wet because of the tear in the
roof-felt that Dad has been going to mend for two years. I couldn't move
it, so I made a careful retreat and managed to shut the door without
disturbing anything dangerous.
15   I went to fetch help. I knew I could have managed if I'd tried harder,
but I never dare stay in our shed for more than a few minutes. I always
remember how it frightened me when I was young. Its two small windows
used to make it look as if it was staring up the garden. It was always full
of noises, squeakings that might be mice, the flapping of the loose felt
20   and, worst of all, the scraping of the twigs of the cedar tree when the
wind moved them across the top of the shed.
Dad came and helped pull the mattress aside. There was still no sign of
the sunbed. I just had to make do with sitting on the grass.

Mark (16)

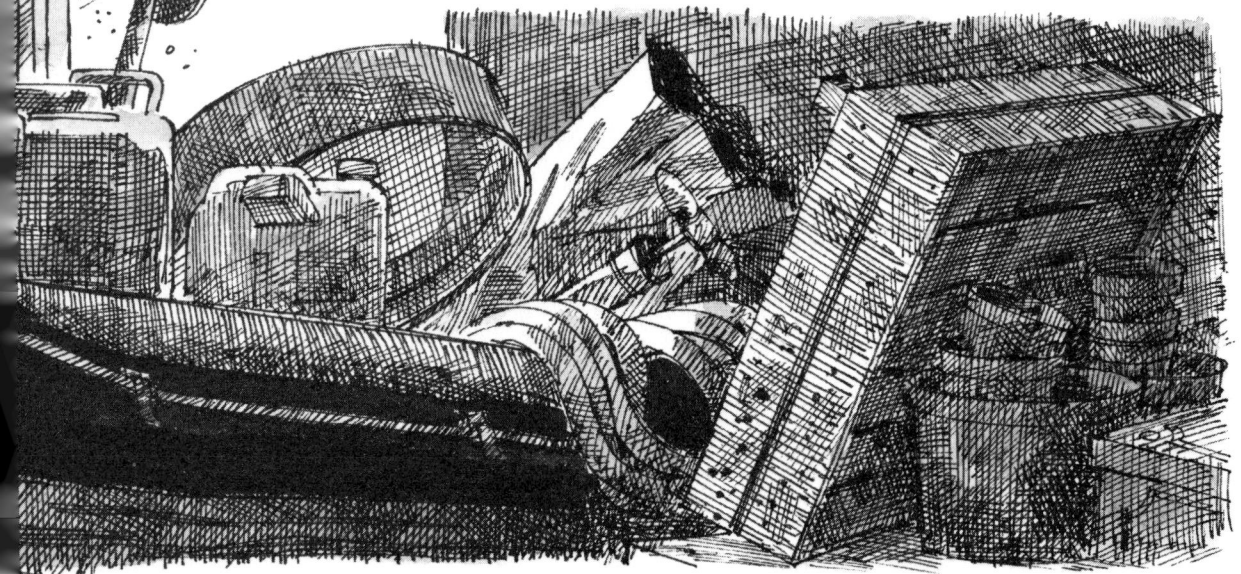

Write your own description

There is nothing unusual about this writer's shed. Most sheds are too full; many have mice and are not in the best state of repair. The sentence structure and vocabulary are quite good, although too many sentences begin with 'I'.

The best feature of this piece of writing is the way the writer shows how he feels about the shed – it is dangerous and frightening.

■ Write about a place well-known to you. Show by the description how you feel about it. What could you write about your main living room, for example.

SELF ASSESSMENT

Read your piece again. Put a pencil line under what you think is the most descriptive sentence.

Understanding

Choose and summarise

Sometimes you are asked to look closely at part of a passage and to pick out the important details.

Tracks

If it hadn't been for the tracks in the snow I doubt whether I should have
ventured far the following morning but they stood out clear; bird tracks,
animal tracks and curious fan-like imprints I hadn't seen before. I am
looking at a sketch of them now. My diaries are not merely the product of
5   nightly homework. Before I set off for the Congo years ago – my first
experience of Africa – a biologist who knew what he was about told me
plainly to write down whatever seemed strange as soon as I saw it. And
sketch in whatever you can, he said. Together with the queries that come
from afterthoughts, all these jottings, the fragments of observation, are
10   transferred to bound notebooks later on.

Outside the garden gate, the dustbin had been overturned for the third
time, the contents scattered in the snow: potato peelings, cabbage leaves,
chicken bones, two bucketsful of fine white wood ash and some beer
cans. When this happened for the first time I put a fairly massive chunk of
15   rock on top of the lid. But some animal had managed to knock it over. If
a dog, it must have been a big one. Two locals occasionally roam about
on the loose, but they are both chained up at night. Annoyed at having
to shovel up widespread garbage yet again, I had jammed the bin under
a ledge in the wall and added another piece of rock. But the creature had
20   managed to knock it over once more. Clearly an opportunity for detection
by snowcraft.

Sheep tracks blurred whatever had happened during the night. I looked
at those small horseshoe-like prints with some misgiving since two beasts
had leaped the wall and gobbled up some of my beloved spring-flowering
25   heathers the previous week. Below the bin, in virgin snow, were the
footmarks of dog and fox; the former with a broader, clearer pad-print
than the more catlike footfalls of the fox, which are usually spaced apart
and in line, one delicate impression almost immediately behind the other.

The clue, if such it was, came from a scurry of prints unknown to me
30   although, when he saw my sketch, Archie the gamekeeper recognised that
animal with long, narrow pads like a small bear. 'Badger,' he said.

from *Journey Through Love* by John Hillaby

47

Find the main facts

■ What had happened to the writer's dustbin and what had he done about it?

The question asks only about the second paragraph of the passage. Read it again, asking What? When? Where? How? questions to pick out the main details and making notes like this:

What had happened to the dustbin?
Overturned. Contents spilt.
When?   Night.
How many times had this happened?   Three times.
What had the writer done the first time?   Put rock on lid.
What had he done the second time?
Jammed bin under ledge. Two rocks on top.
How had the bin been knocked over?   By some creature.
What had the writer done next?   Studied animal tracks round bin.

Summary

'The dustbin had been knocked over for a third time during the night. The first time it had happened, the writer had put a rock on its lid, the second time, he had jammed the bin under a ledge, adding another rock. Now, annoyed by this third upsetting, he studied the tracks round the bin to try to find out which creature had overturned it.'

Notice that:
In a summary you can use one word for a list. The writer mentions 'cabbage leaves', 'chicken bones' among other things. 'Contents' or 'The rubbish' would be enough in a summary. We have not mentioned the contents at all, thinking that a reader might guess there was rubbish in a dustbin.

In a summary, you can miss out the adjectives – the describing words – as a general rule. The first rock on the dustbin was a 'large, massive' one. The summary simply says 'rock' which is enough.

The summary gives the important details. It need not mention what might or might not have happened. This one misses out mention of the dogs who might or might not have disturbed the dustbin.

Choose and summarise for yourself

■ Now read the following story, 'Factory fire'.
■ Then explain in not more than fifty words of your own how the fire started.

48

Factory fire

The factory was making cars. The building was simple and well suited to its purpose. It was long and wide, all on ground level. There were doors at either end, wide enough to let three lorries pass side by side.

5 One summer's day the sun had heated the corrugated steel roof, so the factory was rather warm. Someone opened the doors at one end to let some air in and a strong wind blew straight through the gap. Someone else opened the doors at the other end so that everybody could enjoy the fresh air.

10 In one corner of the works there was an old oil drum which was used for dumping rubbish – paper wrappings soaked in oil, pieces of wood waste, shavings and so on. Somehow this rubbish was set on fire. Nobody knows quite how – perhaps a lighted match was dropped in. Anyway, the smoke billowing out from it was very unpleasant on such a hot day and somebody kicked the drum over to put out the fire.

15 The wind picked up bits of the burning paper and blew them into the paint shop. Paint burns furiously. So does machine oil and there was plenty of that about. Aluminium filings burn even more furiously.

Within minutes, the whole factory was roaring like a furnace. The blaze was whipped up by the wind. Because it was such a simple building, wide
20 open, there was nothing to stop the flames. All the workers had to run for their lives.

from Fire by Leonard Rule

49

SOS – Emergency Services

Fire

Police

Ambulance

Call the operator by dialling 999

or as shown on your telephone number label
or in your dialling instructions

Tell the operator the emergency service you want and
your telephone number (as shown on your telephone)

Wait until the Emergency authority answers

Then give them the full address where help
is needed and other necessary information

Emergency calls to these services are free

For non-urgent calls please consult the alphabetical
directory for the telephone number of the
authority you wish to call. Normal call charges apply.

It is worth remembering how to find 999 in darkness or smoke

We recommend that you get to know the position of the '9' hole or button on your telephone.
Practise trying to find it with your eyes closed as this will help if you have to make
an emergency call in darkness or in a smoke-filled room.

Coastguard

(for coastal and sea rescue)

Cave

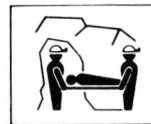

Rescue

Mountain

Rescue

Oral work

Using the telephone

Dial 999

Act this out:

Operator	What service do you require?
Caller	Is that 999?
Operator 1	Yes. What service do you require?
Caller	What do you mean service? A house is on fire!
Operator 1	You want the fire service.
Caller	Yes. For God's sake hurry!
Operator 2	Fire service. What is your telephone number?
Caller	What does that matter?
Operator 2	Your telephone number, please.
Caller	66702.
Operator 2	The exchange, please.
Caller	For God's sake, a house is on fire!
Operator 2	I must have the exchange. It's on the phone above the number.
Caller	Darlaxton.
Operator 2	Where is the fire?
Caller	Just down the road.
Operator 2	The address, please.
Caller	36 Gateshead Road. Hurry. People are trapped.
Operator 2	I'll send an ambulance as well.

■ Now write it out as the caller should have answered and act it out again. Then write phone call plays for these:

An accident to a child cyclist – ambulance.
A break-in at an old person's home – police.
You can act them out sitting back to back.

Spotlight on skills

☆ ☆ ☆ ☆ ☆ ☆ ☆ ☆ ☆ ☆ ☆

Punctuating speech 1

Writing speech in plays is easy because there is no need for speech marks. But using speech in composition needs great care.

'We are going to learn about punctuating speech.'

'That's a good idea.'

Points to watch

1 Use a new line for each new speaker. For instance, with two speakers, use a new line each time one of them says something.
2 If you are not using 'he said' or 'she said' with each speech, write in sentences, beginning with a capital and ending with a full stop. 'I feel very ill.'
3 Put inverted commas ('. . .') at the beginning and end of each speech. 'There is the old man.' Note where the full-stop goes. You can use double or single speech marks. This book uses single.
4 Indent each new speech, that is begin 2–3 centimetres in from the edge of the page.

Write these out

■ There are two speakers and each one speaks twice.

1 We'll go up the M1 as far as Northampton that's a good idea then we take this road through Corby I see

2 Now hand me the screwdriver here you are I'm putting a screw in just here to hang that picture on yes, I think you've got the right place for it

■ There are still two speakers here. Each speaks more than twice.

3 Ranji didn't turn up on Saturday no, he's not very well he was all right on Friday when I saw him yes, but he started with these stomach pains late on Friday night well, give him my best wishes when you see him he'll need more than best wishes because they've taken him to hospital

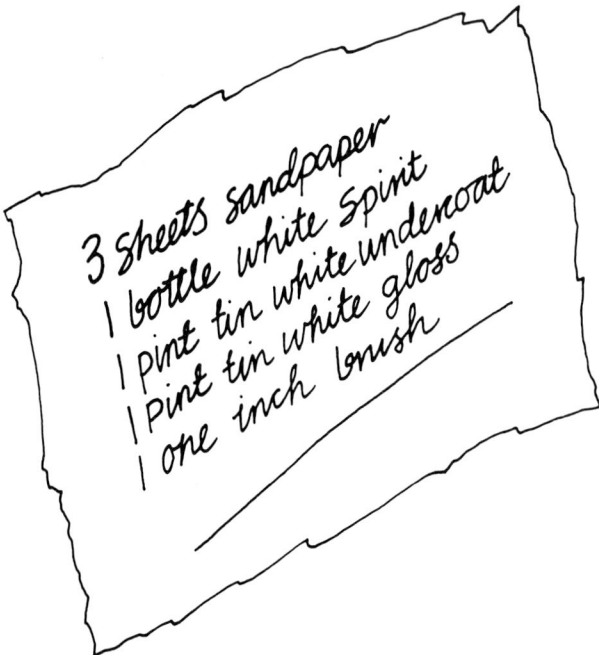

3 sheets sandpaper
1 bottle white spirit
1 pint tin white undercoat
1 pint tin white gloss
1 one inch brush

Communication

Ordering the details

■ If you are reporting a set of facts, you need to set these facts out in a clear and understandable order. Below are five sentences reporting an accident. They are not in the right order. Write them out in an order which gives a clear idea of what happened when and where.

The ambulance, the next to arrive, took the motorcyclist, who was seriously injured, to hospital.

The emergency call went in at 21.08 hours. Police car DZ10 was in the neighbourhood and was first on the scene.

Firemen, arriving almost immediately after the ambulance, needed to use cutting equipment to free the motorist from her vehicle.

An accident between a car and a motorcyclist had occurred on the A 51.

Making notes

A note reminds you of something, using as few words as possible. A person with a painting job may think:

'Well, I've a couple of doors and windows to paint – probably more – so I'll need about a pint of white gloss and undercoat. I'd better get a new brush because that old one's nearly had it. Two inch or one inch? One inch. It's easier to use. Oh, yes and I'm going to need some fresh sandpaper, too. Then I mustn't forget a drop of white spirit for cleaning up and so on. I suppose I'd better write all this down.'

But he or she doesn't write it all down. He or she makes notes of *what* they need.

You answer the phone and the person at the other end says:

'This is Mrs Thomson. Mrs Green has been suddenly taken ill so I'm helping out. I'll be the one picking your mother up tomorrow. She doesn't need to come down to the shopping centre at eight-thirty. I'll call at your house in my car just after nine so will you please tell her to be ready then?'

You can do two things. Trust your memory and get it wrong or write notes like this:

The notes are short answers to questions such as Who? When? Where? How? and – if necessary – Why?

Now make a note

You work in the office of a building firm. A person phones and says:

'This is Mr Nkomo of Beech Grove. Your boss rang me earlier today to ask when it would be convenient to send someone round to fit that new door. Tell him my son will be in all afternoon from about twelve o'clock onwards so he can send someone round any time after that, if that's all right with him.'

■ Make notes of what he said – short answers to questions like:

Who rang?
Where does he live?
What job does he want doing?
When?

Warning about notes

Notes should not be too long. The person with the painting to do would not write:

'I must remember to get three sheets of sandpaper along with a bottle of white spirit and . . .' and so on.
But notes should not be too short, either. Abbreviations – shortened forms of words – are all right but only if they are clear.

'1 wh spir' seems enough to remind a person that he wants 'one bottle of white spirit' but 'Mrs T tom c 9' may not mean much to you if you read it later. You may not remember that 'Mrs T' is Mrs Thomson, 'tom' is tomorrow and 'c' means car.

Notes for reports

If you have to pick out details for a report,
make a note of all the important facts. Then
write the report from your notes. Read the
following:

Break-in

(Neil Riley, at a police station, is confessing to a crime.)

Neil Riley   It wasn't me. It was the other two – Skeg and Cliff –
they led me into it.

Police Officer   Skeg and Cliff?

Neil Riley   Skeg Wilson and Cliff Dean.

Officer   Go on.

Neil Riley   Well, we were out in Cliff's car. It was about one in the
morning. He'd been driving round and round the
buildings where the Seaforth Club was. They'd been
talking about having a giggle and doing some places over
but I wasn't taking much notice. Skeg said there didn't
seem to be anybody about so they parked the car round
the back of the club and went up to the back door. I
followed them just to see what was going on, like. The
door was locked. The other two had a bit of a natter
about what they were going to do and then Cliff got a
brick and broke a window. He put his hand through and
got the window open. We all climbed in. I went because
I was scared of the other two. And I thought – I thought,
if they were trying to go and rob – well – perhaps I
could sort of talk them out of it. Skeg went for the till. I
couldn't see how much he took. He said there was only
about twenty quid. He put the notes and stuff in his
pocket. Cliff was getting some cardboard boxes and
putting bottles of whisky and spirits and all that into
them. We found this full box of bottles of gin. So we
carried all these boxes out to the car and put them in the
boot. Then we – I mean the other two – went back for
some more. We were putting this second load in the boot
when two of your lot came round the corner where
they'd parked the police car and nicked us. It wasn't me,
though. I just went along with the other two because I
didn't want them to do me over. What I did – all I really
did was to go in with them. I just watched. I didn't do
anything. Skeg got the money. I hadn't really anything to
do with the other stuff, either.

Police Officer   All right.

54

You may think that Neil Riley is not telling all the truth. He may be trying to shift the blame on to the other two. That does not matter. All you need for your report – or the statement that Neil Riley might be asked to sign – are the details as he told them.

To make your notes, you might ask questions like this:

What was the name of the place broken into?
At what time did the robbery happen?
What were the names of the men involved?
Who stole from the till?
What else was stolen?
What were they using to carry the stolen goods away in and how were they caught?

Your answers, in note form, may be something like this:

Seaforth Club
About one o'clock in the morning
Three men involved (give names from passage, include speaker)
Till
Skeg Wilson
Other things stolen, bottles of spirits
Cardboard boxes
Men caught by police while loading car

■ Now – from these notes or from the notes you have made for yourself – write your report. Try to keep your report short. It should be no longer than fifty or sixty words.

Step 5

In this Step you are shown how to:

■ write about a picture of a street market.

You are asked to:

■ show how well you understand the argument on a passage called Smoking.

■ discuss in groups what you should and should not be allowed to do in a free country.

■ develop further your use of speech punctuation.

■ write a business letter in the correct manner.

C

Writing

A picture as a starting point

Sometimes, to start you writing in an examination, you are given a picture. It is important to look carefully at the picture and use the details in it for your writing. One way of setting your mind to work is to ask yourself questions about these details. Here is a picture of a street market.

Don't take a quick look and then start writing about 'How I spend Saturday'.

Look carefully at the picture. Take your time.

A story

If you decide to write a story about the picture, here are a few of the things you might ask. You can answer them at this stage in note form.

Who is the main character in your story? The old man in the hat? The stall keeper? The young woman in the duffel coat? The woman with the plastic bag from Boots? One of the other people in the picture?

The old man
Why is he on his own? Has he been married and has his wife died? Or is she ill at home? Or is he married to the woman with the Boots bag? Is he standing aside because he hates shopping? Or has he a definite idea of what he is going to buy and is he looking for the right stall?

The stall keeper
Does she like running a stall? Does she mind the cold? Does she like talking to customers? How does she feel about getting up early to set out the stall?

The woman with the plastic bag from Boots
Is she simply asking the price of the briefs she is holding? Or is she arguing about that? Is she annoyed because the stall keeper isn't paying much attention?

Are you going to write the story from one point of view or will you try to include more than one of the people in the picture?

Your reaction

You may decide to describe your feelings about a street market. These questions can start you off. You can answer them in note form.

What would interest you most about street markets? The colours? The noises? The people? Or the things on sale?
Would you stop to look at any of the stalls you can see in this picture? If so, say why. If not, describe a market stall that would interest you and say why.
Is this picture different from any street market you know? Compare the two.
Do stall keepers interest you? Are some noisy and some quiet in their methods of selling? Give some details.
When did you last visit a street market to buy something? Did you get a bargain or not? What was it?

Give your story a definite shape

Your piece of writing should have a definite shape. It should not be just a list.

Make your story answer a question. Is the old man worried about his wife? Will she get worse? Can he look after her? Is he buying the right things? He talks about his problem to the stall-keeper. Does she cheer him up? When he gets home his wife is better.

If you write about other people, your story might answer questions like this. Is the keeper of the clothes stall worried about money? Does she have a good day in the end? Is it her first day at the market? Is it a success? What happens to make it a success or not?

If you write about several people in the picture, connect up their stories.
You could do this by having them chat to each other as they wander about and meet in the market.

Make sure your reaction has a pattern

Give this piece of writing a pattern too. You could start by saying whether you like markets or not. Do you like or dislike the one in the picture?
Use the details in the picture to explain why you like or dislike the place. You could compare this one to another street market you know. Is there a particular stall in a market that always interests you? Describe what you see on it and explain your interest. Do you have a particular memory of something that happened or something you saw in a market? You could finish the piece of writing with a highlight like that.

■ Now either write a story about the market or your reactions to street markets, or a story about another picture.

SELF ASSESSMENT

Exchange with a neighbour and check how you have both done any speech punctuation. Underline with a pencil anything that does not sound like real speech.

Understanding

Picking out the points of an argument

Passages which put forward an argument do it point by point. Questions may be set to see whether you can follow the line of an argument closely. You may also be asked to look at the passage paragraph by paragraph and summarise the points in your own words. Read the following and answer the question.

Smoking

How much money would you spend each week to poison yourself? Silly question? If you smoke, you are doing just that. Smoking costs money and however much you spend on cigarettes, you are spending it on something harmful.

Or does the question make you smile? There is nothing funny about an early death from bronchitis, heart disease or lung cancer. As it says on the packets, 'Smoking can seriously damage your health'. How often, as you light up and inhale, do you think about that? Have you ever thought of giving up smoking? Have you ever tried to stop?

Find three reasons

■ The passage gives three main reasons for stopping smoking. Explain, in a sentence for each, what these three reasons are. Use, as far as you can, your own words in your answer.

Oral work

Discussion

■ Listed below are actions that some people think are a person's own business; they should be allowed because they don't harm other innocent people. Divide them into three lists.

1 The actions you are free to do without breaking the law.
2 The actions you may do if you are given permission by authorities.
3 The actions that are against the law.

    Build extra rooms on your house
    Commit suicide
    Smoke
    Drive a car without seatbelts
    Walk down the street naked
    Drink alcohol
    Take drugs
    Marry two wives or two husbands
    Own a gun
    Keep a tiger in your garden
    Walk on a motorway
    Not send your children to school
    Fight in the street (with someone who is willing)
    Assault a burglar who has broken into your house
    Bury one of your family in the garden

■ Decide what changes you would make in the list. For instance, you might make smoking against the law and allow people not to send their children to school.

Discussion in groups of four

■ Divide into groups of four. Discuss your changes. Remember to give reasons.

■ Pick a spokesperson. Let each group spokesperson present the group's views to the rest of the class.

■ Vote on changes as a class.

Spotlight on skills

☆ ☆ ☆ ☆ ☆ ☆ ☆ ☆ ☆ ☆ ☆

Speech punctuation 2

When using phrases like 'he said' or 'Linda told them' or 'The old lady said' at the end of a speech, you do not end that speech with a full stop. Use a comma instead, like this:
    'We were looking for you,' Debbie said.
Put the full stop after '. . . said.'

For a question, use a question mark after the speech, like this:
    'Where did you lose it?' Michael asked.

Use an exclamation mark in the same way when it is needed, like this:
    'Catch that dog!' the farmer yelled.

■ Write this out. (You will need to use one exclamation mark and three question marks.)

1 Rob Keith called he isn't here Susan said where is he, then Keith asked how should I know she said he was supposed to wait for us here at ten o'clock Keith grumbled perhaps he's gone on to the bus stop Susan said shall we go and look for him there Lyn asked I suppose so Keith said

You will need to remember all the points about speech punctuation for this. Some capitals are missing, too.

2 ow said Salim what's the matter Carmen asked i've just fallen over a chair he told her well, why don't you switch the light on she asked where's the switch over by the door, of course i've got it he told her that's better she said, as the light came on

60

Communication

Business letters

The boxes below show how a business letter should be set out.

Reference number if you have already had a letter from the company

Your address including postcode

Your telephone number

The address of the company you are writing to

The date

Dear Sir – if you are writing to the company for the first time

Dear Mr, Mrs, Ms or Miss – if you know the person you are writing to

Slightly inset the beginning of your letter

Yours sincerely – if you have written to a person by name

Yours faithfully – if you used 'Dear Sir' above

Your signature

Study the way this business letter is set out.

```
                                      10 Green Street
                                      Haslington
   Your ref:                          York
   MS/YP/75603                         YO4 8RF
   7 August 1986                       Tel: York 67544


   Mr Singh                               9 August 86
   Express Printing Works
   Ryman's Row
   York
   YO1 9EG


   Dear Mr Singh
        Thank you for your letter. It was good of you to reply
   so quickly.

        I will accept your offer to visit your printing works
   on Thursday, the 10th of September at 3p.m.

        I would be grateful for any examples of your work you
   could let me have for my project.


   Yours sincerely
   Jane Welbourne
```

NB: This is the unpunctuated style of letter.

■ Set out the beginnings and endings of the letters. You do not have to write the letter.

1 Tom Anderson lives at 104, Welby Gardens, North Road, Stevenage, Herts, and is writing to Helen Morris, the manager of Penton Office Equipment Ltd. The office is at 37, The Precinct, Manchester M7 4BJ. Mr Anderson has already received a letter from Miss Morris dated the 12th July, with the reference number RV/279. The postcode for Welby Gardens is SG1 2JE.

2 Paul Grossett of 35, Burleigh Grove, Gorlton, Chelmsford, is writing to a company called Four Seasons Boat Hire of Waterside Road, Bacton, Suffolk. Paul's postcode is CM9 3TB. This is the first time he has written to the company.

Write a complete letter

■ Write to Conway Garden Centre to order six roses. Their address is 45, Ninton Road, Buckland, Saltshire, BD2 4XL. The catalogue entry for the roses you want is:

Nuits de Young: Height 5 ft. Spread 3ft – velvety double flowers, maroon purple. Cat. no. 8003 – Price: £1.20 each

At the bottom of the catalogue is printed:

When ordering please quote catalogue number. Cheques/postal orders should be made payable to 'Conway Garden Centre Ltd'. Postage and packing: a surcharge of 75p is necessary to cover postage and packing for orders under £10.

Before you write your letter study this one.

19, Enver Way,
Coton,
Lepshire.

LE92 3EN

Conway Garden Centre,
45, Ninton Road,
Buckland
BD2 4XL

Dear Sir,
    I wish to order six Nuits de Young roses and I enclose a cheque for £7.20.

Yours sincerely,

Mr. Ian Dobson

What has been missed out?
What mistakes have been made?
Discuss which style your teacher would like, the punctuated or the unpunctuated.

Step 6

In this step you are shown how to:

■ build your writing to a climax.

■ give an eye-witness report.

■ cope with multiple choice questions on the *Weather* and *The mugger.*

You are asked to:

■ check your use of capitals.

■ write a reply to a letter of complaint.

■ take a role in a telephone conversation.

Writing

Hiroshima

Before six o'clock that morning, Mr Tanimoto started for Mr Matsuo's
house. There he found that their burden was to be a tansu, a large
Japanese cabinet, full of clothing and household goods. The two men set
out. The morning was perfectly clear and so warm that the day promised
5 to be uncomfortable. A few minutes after they started, the air-raid siren
went off – a minute-long blast that warned of approaching planes but
indicated to the people of Hiroshima only a slight degree of danger, since
it sounded every morning at that time, when an American weather plane
came over.

10 The two men pushed and pulled the handcart through the city streets.
Hiroshima was a fan-shaped city, lying mostly on the six islands formed
by the seven estuarial rivers that branch out from the Ota River; its main
commercial and residential districts, covering about four square miles in
the centre of the city, contained three-quarters of its population, which
15 had been reduced by several evacuation programmes from a wartime
peak of 380,000 to about 245,000. Factories and other residential
districts, or suburbs, lay compactly around the edges of the city. To the
south were the docks, an airport, and the island-studded Inland Sea. A
rim of mountains runs around the other three sides of the delta.

20 Mr Tanimoto and Mr Matsuo took their way through the shopping centre,
already full of people, and across two of the rivers to the sloping streets
of Koi, and up them to the outskirts and the foothills. As they started up
a valley away from the tight-ranked houses, the all-clear sounded. (The
Japanese radar operators, detecting only three planes, supposed that they
25 comprised a reconnaissance.) Pushing the handcart up to the rayon man's
house was tiring, and the men, after they had manoeuvred their load into
the driveway and to the front steps, paused to rest a while. They stood
with a wing of the house between them and the city. Like most homes in
this part of Japan, the house consisted of a wooden frame and wooden
30 walls supporting a heavy tile roof. Its front hall, packed with rolls of
bedding clothing, looked a cool cave full of fat cushions. Opposite the
house, to the right of the front door, there was a large, finicky rock
garden. There was no sound of planes. The morning was still; the place
was cool and pleasant.

35 Then a tremendous flash of light cut across the sky. Mr Tanimoto had a
distinct recollection that it travelled from east to west, from the city toward
the hills. It seemed a sheet of sun. Both he and Mr Matsuo reacted in
terror – and both had time to react (for they were 3500 yards, or two

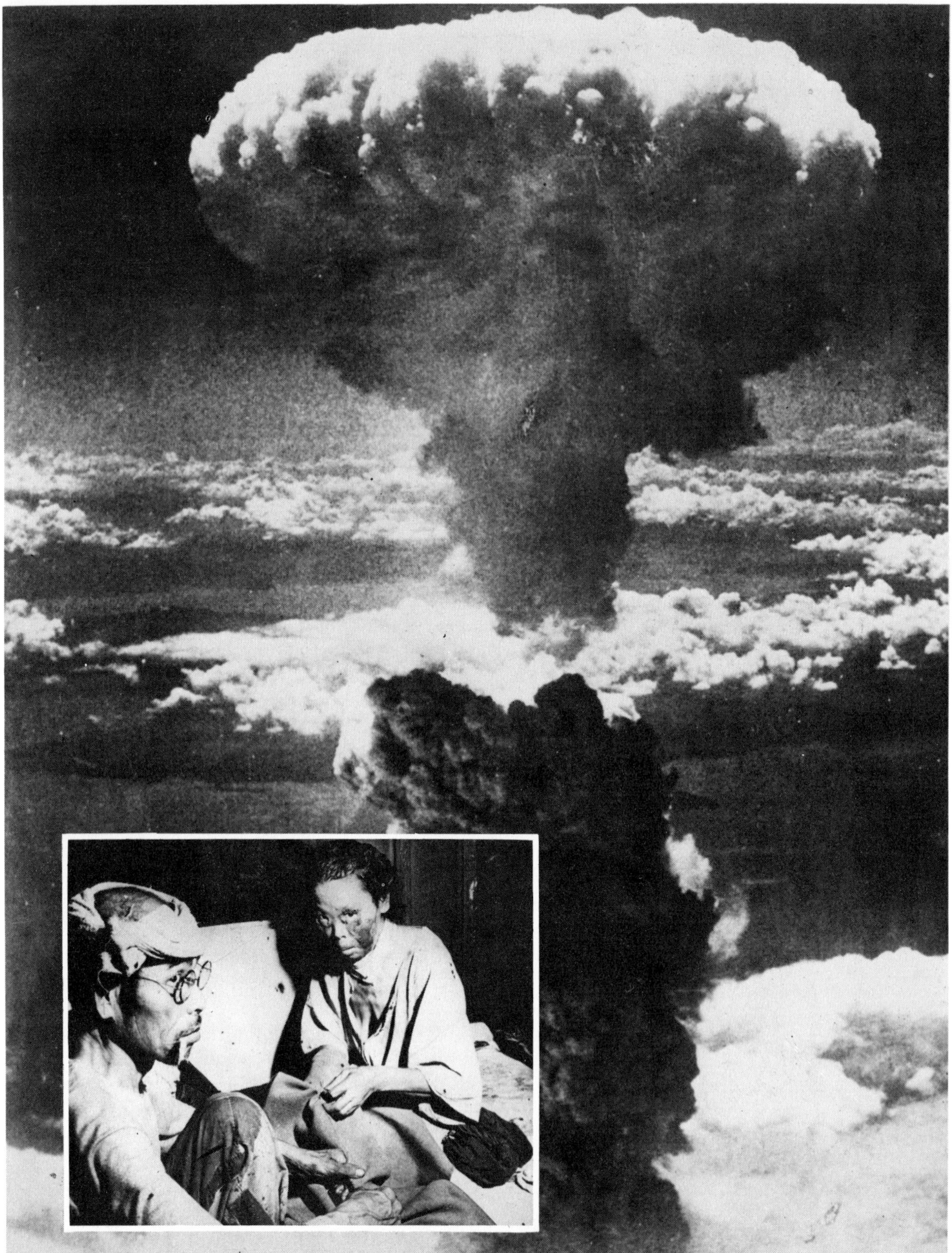

miles, from the centre of the explosion). Mr Matsuo dashed up the front
40 steps of the house and dived among the bed rolls and buried himself
there. Mr Tanimoto took four or five steps and threw himself between two
big rocks in the garden. He bellied up very hard against one of them. As
his face was against the stone, he did not see what happened. He felt a
sudden pressure, and then splinters and pieces of board and fragments of
45 tile fell on him. He heard no roar. (Almost no one in Hiroshima recalls
hearing any noise of the bomb. But a fisherman in his sampan on the
Inland Sea near Tsuzu, the man with whom Mr Tanimoto's mother-in-law
and sister-in-law were living, saw the flash and heard a tremendous
explosion; he was nearly twenty miles from Hiroshima, but the thunder
50 was greater than when the B-29's hit Iwakuni, only five miles away.)

When he dared, Mr Tanimoto raised his head and saw that the rayon
man's house had collapsed. He thought a bomb had fallen directly on it.
Such clouds of dust had risen that there was a sort of twilight around. In
panic, not thinking for the moment of Mr Matsuo under the ruins, he
55 dashed out into the street. He noticed as he ran that the concrete wall of
the estate had fallen over toward the house rather than away from it. In
the street, the first thing he saw was a squad of soldiers who had been
burrowing into the hillside opposite, making one of the thousands of
dugouts in which the Japanese apparently intended to resist invasion, hill
60 by hill, life for life; the soldiers were coming out of the hole, where they
should have been safe, and blood was running from their heads, chests,
and backs. They were silent and dazed.

Under what seemed to be a local dust cloud, the day grew darker and
darker.

from *Hiroshima* by John Hersey

Building to a climax

Look at this piece of writing carefully. It is an account of the dropping of the first atomic bomb on the city of Hiroshima in Japan in 1945.

Read it first to get the story out of it.

Then think why the author has written it in the way he has done. He has carefully built up his writing so that the maximum effect is obtained when the bomb is dropped. He then uses eye-witness accounts to show at first-hand what it was like to be in an atomic explosion.

John Hersey could have written:

Two men were working in a Japanese city. There was a big flash of light. A lot of damage was done.

Instead he gave a much fuller account.

■ Answer the questions on page 68 to help you understand the skill of his writing.

1 What sets the peaceful tone at the beginning of the passage?
2 What, briefly, disturbs that peace?
3 What hints are there that something dreadful is about to happen? Why, for instance, does the author mention the construction of the buildings?
4 What makes Hiroshima like any other city? Is this important to the way the account is written?
5 What makes Mr Tanimoto and Mr Matsuo like ordinary people? Why might the author have stressed this?
6 What do you gather about the size of the town? Is this important to the account?
7 Why does the author end paragraph three with those particular last two sentences?

8 What is immediately horrific about the bomb?
9 What was odd about the explosion as it was so great?
10 How does the author show it was a great explosion?
11 Do the two men react in the way you would expect?
12 Why is the observation about what happened to the soldiers important and how does it show this was not a normal explosion?
13 Why has the writer put in the last, single sentence paragraph?

Your own writing

You are walking along a peaceful canal bank. You see people fishing and small children. The day is hot and close. A child, playing on the bridge, falls in. There is immediate activity as the rescue attempt is made. The rescue is not helped by a sudden fall of heavy rain in a thunderstorm.

■ Write two contrasting paragraphs. One of peace; the other of activity and noise.
   Put in small details. You might mention butterflies in the first paragraph, for instance.
   Make up a title for your piece of writing when you have finished it.
   You should do 150 words or more for the first paragraph and 200 words or more for the second.

SELF ASSESSMENT

Make a list of the words you have used which suggest peace. Do you know which are adjectives? Mark them 'A' if you do.

Eye-witness account

■ Write an account of the most odd thing that happened to you or that you saw. Make it sound true by putting in as much detail as possible.

or

If nothing of the kind has ever happened to you, make up an account of an accident you could witness.

or

Use the picture above to write an eye-witness account of a ghostly event that took place in this house. In the piece you select give details of: time of day, place, weather, names of people, etc.

SELF ASSESSMENT

Exchange with two neighbours. Who has written the most true sounding account? Do not say if yours is really true.

Understanding

Multiple choice questions

In multiple choice questions, you are given a selection of answers and asked to pick the right one. Read the next short passage and the explanation that follows.

Weather

Weather forecasts on the radio, on television or in newspapers are the work of this country's Meteorological Office. This Office gathers and examines all kinds of weather signs, wind speed, temperature, air pressure, and then predicts the weather. Nearly everyone, a farmer, a soldier, a sailor, a business person or even a person planning a picnic, depends to some extent on these weather forecasts.

The Meteorological or 'Met' Office keeps full records of what the weather patterns have been in the past. It is in touch with other weather-forecasting services in many other countries and uses all kinds of equipment from high-altitude balloons to computers to do its job.

Remember: all kinds of multiple choice questions may be set on a passage. There are two things that will help you to get your answers right.

1 Be sure you know what the question is asking for. Read it carefully and think about it.

2 In the answers listed, some may be **nearly right** or **near enough**. Only one is **exactly right**. Pick the only one that is exactly right.

Here are some types of question that might be asked about the passage on weather. They are followed by an explanation of why only one answer is exactly right.

1 Which of these words is closest in meaning to the word **predicts** in the passage?

wonders
guesses
forecasts
decides

The weather forecasters are not wondering or guessing what the weather is going to be like. They have plenty of evidence and they are working from that, so the answers **wonders** and **guesses** are not right.
You are left with **decides** and **forecasts**. Forecasts is nearest to the meaning of predicts so it is the exactly right answer.

2 What signs used to foretell weather are **not** mentioned in the passage?
air pressure
rainfall
temperature
wind speed

Here you will get the right answer if you have read the question carefully. It asks for something **not** in the passage. Air pressure, temperature, and wind speed are all mentioned in the passage. Rainfall is **not** mentioned, so it is the correct answer.

3 What equipment used in weather forecasting is mentioned in the passage?

weather patterns in the past
weather information from other countries
balloons and thermometers
computers and balloons

If you read the question carefully, you will notice that it asks for 'equipment'. **Weather patterns in the past** and **weather information from other countries** are both mentioned in the passage but neither of these is 'equipment'. The two things mentioned at the end of the passage are equipment. Again, read the passage carefully. **Balloons and computers** are mentioned. **Thermometers** are not. You need both balloons and computers in the answer, so, this answer is exactly right.

So far we have looked at one or two types of question. You will meet questions like this again, after the next passage but they are set in the form of multiple choice questions.

The mugger

Kennedy was a large man with a short temper who believed in keeping fit. Every morning he would go for a three mile run round the park.

The particular morning he was half way round his course when another man, also a runner, rounded a corner and bumped into him, sending
5   Kennedy staggering. Gasping a short apology, the second man ran on. Kennedy glared after him. Then he felt for his wallet.

The wallet had gone. Kennedy's suspicions were confirmed. His pocket had been picked. Furious, he chased after the robber. Running hard, Kennedy overhauled the pickpocket and stopped him in his tracks.
10   Kennedy scowled. The robber was a much smaller man.

'Right!' snarled Kennedy. 'Let's have it! Hand over the wallet!' The man went pale, gulped and handed it over without a word. Then he ran off as fast as he could.

Kennedy did not follow. He had what he wanted. There was his wallet,
15   brown, with a zip, safely back in his hand. He slipped it back into his pocket and puffed off to complete his fitness training.

When he got home, however, he was in for a surprise. There was his wallet, lying where he had left it before he started his morning run. It looked identical to the one he had taken from the man in the park. It was
20   on top of the chest of drawers in his bedroom where it had been all the time. Much embarrassed, Kennedy opened the other wallet. Quite obviously it belonged to the man who had bumped into him. Fortunately, however, it had the man's telephone number in it. Kennedy rang him to apologise. He arranged a time and a place to hand the thing back to its owner.
25   'I'm very sorry about all this,' Kennedy said again at last. 'But — why didn't you tell me that it was your wallet?'

'I thought you were going to mug me,' the voice on the phone told him. 'I've heard that the worst thing you can do, if someone threatens to mug you, is to put up a fight. So I gave you my wallet.'

Questions on the mugger

■ Write down the number of each question and against it the letter of the answer you think is the correct one. There is only one correct answer for each question.

1 Which of these is nearest in meaning to **gasping** in the second paragraph?

   a muttering quietly
   b breathing deeply
   c trying to protest
   d struggling for breath   (1)

2 About how far had Kennedy run when the other man bumped into him?

   a one mile
   b three miles
   c one and a half miles
   d half a mile   (1)

3 Kennedy ran after the other man because he thought the man was:

   a very clumsy
   b a mugger
   c a pickpocket
   d a much smaller man.   (1)

4 After he had handed over the wallet, the smaller man ran off because:

   a he was late
   b he was afraid of Kennedy
   c he thought Kennedy might call the police
   d he wanted to finish his training run. (1)

5 Kennedy did not follow the smaller man as he ran off because Kennedy:

   a had got his wallet back
   b did not want any more trouble
   c was tired
   d was out of breath.   (1)

6 Which two words best describe how Kennedy felt when he found his own wallet at home?

   a surprised and amused
   b surprised and embarrassed
   c much embarrassed
   d embarrassed and angry   (1)

7 Which two words are nearest in meaning to **identical to** in the sixth paragraph?

   a very like
   b exactly like
   c quite like
   d similar to   (1)

8 Kennedy was able to contact the other man again because:

   a he found the man's number in a telephone book
   b he found the man's telephone number in the wallet
   c the man called round to see him
   d the man found Kennedy's telephone number.   (1)

9 The man had handed over his wallet without argument because:

   a he thought it was Kennedy's wallet
   b he had stolen the wallet from Kennedy
   c he did not know what to say
   d he thought Kennedy might beat him up.   (1)

10 Summarise in your own words and as briefly as you can what happened when Kennedy got home.   (5)

Spotlight on skills

☆ ☆ ☆ ☆ ☆ ☆ ☆ ☆ ☆ ☆ ☆

Using capitals

A certain place has its own special name. So does a person. That name is written with a capital letter. Names, nicknames, streets, roads, towns, counties, countries, all begin with a capital letter.

Edinburgh St

Italy *Manchester*

Natasha *Kent*

■ Write this out, putting in all the missing capitals.

Mrs robson, who lives in oak road, in our town, bronfield, went on a tour of england last year in her car. Her daughter jane, went with her. So did her son, ian, nicknamed robbo. They visited oxford, bristol and stafford and then went up to cumbria. From there they first went north and then into yorkshire to stay for a few days in york. Mrs robson comes from the south and likes the southern counties such as kent, surrey and sussex but jane and ian preferred the moors and hills of lancashire and northumbria

Last year the robsons had a motoring holiday in france and germany but they all said that their two weeks in britain had been just as enjoyable.

When you write the days of the week, the months of the year or special days of the year, you begin with a capital letter.

Tuesday	January
Wednesday	February
Saturday	August

NB: the seasons are small letters, for example spring, summer.

■ Write out the days of the week. Check that you have got the spelling right.

■ Write out the months of the year. Check that you have spelt these months correctly.

■ Five of these do not start with a capital letter. Write out only the days that start with a capital.

new year's day   today   may day   easter
good friday   tomorrow   whitsuntide
yesterday   august bank holiday   hallowe'en
guy fawkes' day   birthday   christmas day
holiday   boxing day

Communication

A letter of complaint

Imagine that the roses you received from your order on page 63 were planted on October 4th and the following June they bloom yellow instead of maroon. You have yellow roses already and want the maroon ones as a contrast.

■ Write a letter to Conway Garden Centre, explaining what has happened and asking for your money to be refunded. Include details of the date you ordered and received the roses, the name and catalogue number.

Answer a letter

Exchange letters with your neighbour. You now change roles. You are the secretary to Ann Johnson, who is in overall charge of distribution at Conway Garden Centre. You show her the letter of complaint. She looks in the file and finds that the roses sent were 'Chicago Peace', catalogue number 8008. She says:

'It's probably Bob's fault. I've told him before not to just go by the catalogue number. You can easily make a mistake, especially if the writing is bad. But we're not going to refund any money. She (or he) has had the roses for over six months. It clearly states in our brochure that mistakes can't be rectified after three months. Yes, I know she (he) didn't know the colour until they bloomed, but we send a leaflet with every order, asking customers to check the name and catalogue number on receipt of the goods. You'd better write saying we're sorry but pointing out that it's too late to refund money. I know, send a free sample of that new rose 'Baron Flame' – we don't want to offend customers but they really must read the catalogue more carefully. Oh, and you'd better send a memo to Bob, telling him what's happened and asking him to keep a more careful check.'

■ Write the reply to your neighbour's letter. When you have finished exchange letters again.
Are you satisfied with the reply? Does it sound fair?

Consider this letter. Notice the first line. You should always acknowledge receipt of a previous letter in this way.
What needs to be left out of paragraph one?

■ Paragraph two is the weakness of the letter. Rewrite it. What else is wrong?

Conway Garden Centre,
45, Ninton Road,
Buckland,
Salts.

13.7.86

Dear Miss Wills,
        Thank you for your letter dated 21st June. We are sorry to hear about the mistake over the roses. We think there was a mistake over the catalogue number because of your terrible writing.

    We are sorry we cannot refund your money because you have waited such a long time before complaining.

    We are sending you a sample of our latest rose called 'Baron Flame'. We hope that you will continue as a customer.

            Yours sincerely,

            Ann Johnson

            Manager

NB: This is the punctuated style of letter.

Oral work

A telephone conversation

■ Imagine you are not satisfied with the company's reply. Ring the manager (your neighbour – you can change roles later). Ask again if you can have your money refunded.

It makes the situation more realistic if you actually mime holding a telephone and do not look at each other during the conversation.

Do not be rude. Do not make vague threats ('I'll sue you.'). Discuss the matter calmly but make your points firmly. There is no winner or loser – you are both acting parts.

Step 7

In this Step you are shown how to:

- use comparisons to help your reader understand an unusual experience.

- judge a piece of writing by a pupil.

- draw conclusions on a passage about a wedding party in Spain.

You are asked to:

- study the difference between formal and informal writing.

- prepare a talk for taping or giving to the whole class.

- check further the use of capital letters.

- make notes for reports of a mysterious event and an accident.

Writing

The mill

Yesterday's footprints lay clear in the flour-like dust. His own, with ribbed soles; Mum's pointed ones; Jane's little ones; Joe Moreton's elephantine ones. He walked round wiping out Joe's footprints with a twist of his foot, wherever he could find them.

5   The vertical main drive-shaft caught his eye, with the great grinding millstone at the bottom. An octagonal oak pillar, with a huge wooden cog fastened horizontally across the top. Struts went up from the shaft to support the cog diagonally, like the diagonal strut on a gallows. But he was far more interested in the way the cog fitted into the next cog, which

10   fitted into the next shaft, which had another cog . . . . He began to understand how the mill worked. Understanding, he climbed slowly up-wards to the very top platform.

    There, he found a big wooden lever; whitewashed below, but rounded and black above, with the grease of the miller's hand. He put his hand to

15   it; it fitted his hand so perfectly, like a sword he'd once picked up in the Tower of London and been told off for. Something made him pull the lever gently towards him. It seemed the thing to do, somehow.

    There came a faint sour-sweet smell: the smell of rain hitting dry summer dust; a smell he'd always loved. It came from a long wooden

20   trough running past him. As he looked, the floor of the trough changed from rough wood to shining blackness.

    Water was running into the mill. All over, different sounds of rushing waters, like little waterfalls.

    Then the noise of a dustbin being rolled by bin-men, right beneath his

25   feet. A dustbin two inches thick . . . .

    Then *tong . . . tong . . . tong tong tong tong tong* – a noise like a boy rattling an iron bar along iron railings.

    The whole mill began to vibrate gently up through the soles of his training-shoes.

30   Entranced, he moved about. The sounds changed as he moved. Went deeper. Roaring, like a lion, chained up underground. Water going *shee-shee-shee*, like a heart beating. Rumbles like indigestion inside his own body, so deep-down were they. Again, *shee-shee-shee*, like the blood pounding in his own ears.

35   But the mill didn't run evenly, like a vacuum cleaner. It varied like a living thing. In the long wooden trough, the water surged deep for a few seconds, then shallow again. The machinery would run quietly for a while, then break out with a violent chatter of gears. Even the quiet-and-loud patches were never quite the same length. You could never get *used* to

40   them; you had to listen carefully for *every* change, because it was new.

You could go on listening forever. He wandered slowly down the narrow stairs and gangways, over the throbbing pits. It *was* like being inside a clock. Segments of wheels turning in the grey light from the still-open window; then spinning off into pitch darkness. The thick grease on
45   the cogwheels was like blue-black butter.

     The inside of a great drum, with a dozen drummers playing, loud and soft, near and far. But the biggest drummer was still lower, beneath his feet.

     Down, down, he went. To where the brick of the walls sweated. And
50   the white roots of plants pushed down through the brick arch overhead: tried vainly to curl back up, back into the brick from whence they came:

but they never would, they'd just hang helpless forever in the dark. The only homely thing was the lettering on the bricks, which said the name of a firm in Manchester.

55   He was near now. Near to the biggest drummer. And then, in the last ghost of light, he saw it: the huge water-wheel, redleaded turning in its tomb of black stone, turning, turning slowly; leaking water like a rainstorm, sometimes throwing down whole sheets. The metal of the axle, inside the huge rumbling noise, whimpered like a small hurt animal; or

60 chirruped like a canary. The wheel was barnacled with rust, like a rock at low tide.

    All these sounds the miller must have known; been deafened by for years. Or did he get so used to them that he could still pick out the softest footfall behind him . . .?

65   Simon whirled in terror.

    There was nothing there. But he knew that if there had been a footstep, *he* wouldn't have heard it. Soaked with sweat and spray, he ran, and did not stop running till he was again on the topmost platform, panting. He pushed the starting lever back the way it had come.

70   from *The Scarecrows* by Robert Westall

Comparisons

The mill is full of unusual sights, sounds and smells. The writer uses comparisons that we are familiar with to give us the impression of the mill as it begins to work.

■ Find the comparisons that help us understand these and write them out.

1 The smell created as the water fills the floury and dusty trough.
2 The sounds of water beginning to flood into various parts of the mill.
3 The rattling noise that began right under the boy's feet.
4 The deep rumbling noises.
5 The complicated movement and noise of cogwheels.
6 The appearance of the grease on the cogwheels.

The writer says 'the only homely thing was the lettering on the bricks', but he has tried to make the strange sounds and sights of the mill more understandable to the reader by comparing them with familiar things.

80

Read Cathy's description of a new and frightening experience. She has been given a course of six riding lessons as a birthday present. Cathy is fifteen, but is recalling what happened when she was seven.

A frightening experience

My mother waved and drove off, leaving me surrounded by large farm buildings, dilapidated wooden sheds, gates and dirt-tracks leading off in all directions. Nervously I made my way to a door marked 'Stable Office'. The door creaked as I pushed it open and I was suddenly in a room so
5   dingy that I thought at first there were no windows, but after a few seconds I could see well enough by the light that struggled through the filthy panes to make out the huge, dark saddles and bridles hanging round the walls. The atmosphere was stuffy and the air was thick with dust. There was a strong smell like rotting grass.

10   A wooden partition about four feet high marked the far end of the room. I was just getting used to the gloom and the smell when there was a rustling from behind the partition, a sound like rats moving about in straw. I was too terrified even to run. Then a horse's head poked over the partition. It wrinkled its nose and sneezed, showing big spiky teeth as
15   yellow as butter. I stared up at the head, fascinated as well as terrified. Its eyes looked a friendly deep brown, but shiny liquid, like spit, ran down from them nearly as far as its nose.
      'Name?' said a deep voice behind me. I jumped nearly as high as the horse's head, turned round and found myself looking at a huge woman
20   with fiery red hair, squinty eyes and a scowling face. Her dirty red anorak was stretched over three jumpers. She stood with her fat legs wide apart.
      'Name?' she repeated.
      'Cathy Geeson,' I managed to reply in a tiny squeaking voice.
25   'Come with me,' she thundered and strode out of the creaking door. I had to run to keep up with her.

Fortunately the pony called Toby looked small and innocent. I felt better until the woman said 'Mount!' Of course I hadn't any idea of how to climb onto Toby, but I hadn't time to protest before I felt the grip of
30   masculine hands on my shoulders. She hoisted me on and slotted my feet into the stirrups.

The next half hour was a nightmare. The ground seemed so distant. I knew I would break my neck if I fell. The huge woman boomed orders that I didn't understand. I became more tense the more she shouted. She
35   dragged the pony round as if she was pulling for a tug-of-war team. When she eventually dragged me off my legs were so trembly I could hardly stand. That was my first and last riding lesson. I refused to go for the other five.

Cathy (15)

Write comments on Cathy's impressions

Cathy was frightened of:

The stable office
The horse behind the partition
The instructor

■ Write a four line comment on each, saying how successfully she has described her fear.

Find the comparisons

■ Cathy has used five comparisons to help describe her strange and frightening experience. Pick them out and write a comment on each. Do they help your understanding? Which ones are successful in the same way as those in the windmill passage, comparing something unusual with something familiar?

Write your own description

■ Write a description of an unusual place you have visited. It can be pleasant or unpleasant. Your main description should be of the place itself but, like Cathy, you may include people. Remember to record your feelings. Write at least 350 words.

SELF ASSESSMENT

Read your piece again. Underline in pencil any sentences that really show your feelings.

Understanding

Drawing your own conclusions

Some passages do not state facts directly. In places they hint at things. They let you draw your own conclusions from the evidence given. In cases like that you have to be aware of clues that are given. Questions are sometimes set to see how good you are at spotting these hints and clues and seeing what they mean.

■ Read the following passage and then answer the questions that follow it.

A wedding party in Spain

Later that evening I walked the streets alone, too bright with wine to feel the need for sleep. There was a curious music in the air and a stamping of feet in the darkness and as I stood in the plaza an army of young men suddenly appeared and came marching towards me, singing lustily. They were bearing guitars, mandolines, cymbals, flutes and drums of pigskin which growled when you stroked them.

'We are going to a wedding,' cried the leader and invited me to go with them. Very glad of a wedding on such a night, I accepted without hesitation. I was given a pigskin drum to stroke and I fell in behind and we all marched away to the fisherman's suburb, playing loudly as we went.

It was a warm, dark winter night and the season for serenading was in full swing. On every hand the town was alive with it. Women and children leaned out of the rose-red windows to watch us as we passed by. We began to meet other bands marching and counter-marching about the town. Sometimes they crossed our paths with hideous discord and then just faded away into the darkness. At others, they met us head on in narrow streets and no one would give way and then what stiff-necked rivalry there was, what tightening of strings and jutting of jaws, what glorious bedlam as we all stood breast to breast, sweating and thumping our instruments and each trying to outplay the other.

from *A Rose for Winter* by Laurie Lee

1 How do you know that, before he met the band, the writer had had a few drinks which had made him feel quite lively? (2)
2 What tells you that the sound of the pig-skin drum reminded him of an animal? (2)
3 What suggests that he had nothing much to do that evening before he met the band? (2)
4 In what part of the town was the wedding most probably going to be held? (2)
5 What suggests that all the different bands were playing different tunes? (2)
6 How can you tell that the town can't have had many cars or lorries or other traffic moving about? (2)

Oral work

Here are two short extracts from two letters. One is an informal letter to a relative, asking for the return of some shoes. The other is a more formal letter to the manager of a hotel, also about shoes.

A

. . . I've left a pair of shoes under my bed. I think that's where they are. I was in such a rush, I forgot them. Can you post them on to me? I need them this weekend. If they're not under the bed, they're somewhere about in that back bedroom . . .

B

. . . When vacating my room, I unfortunately left behind a pair of brown shoes. I would be much obliged if they could be posted on to me. I should, naturally, be quite willing to pay the cost of postage. Thanking you in anticipation . . . .

■ Which is the informal letter to the relative? Which is the formal letter to the hotel manager? How did you decide? Give reasons.

When writing to someone you know well, use language that is fairly simple and relaxed. When writing to a stranger, such as the manager of a firm or a hotel manager, language is more formal.

Chatting or giving a talk

When chatting to friends, use language that is simple and relaxed. When giving a talk, use more formal language.

Here are two more short extracts. One is from a conversation about keeping a dog. The other is from a talk to an audience on the same subject.

C

. . . Well, you – er – take them for walks for one thing. You've – sort of – got to look after them in all sorts of ways. I mean, there's walks and then there's – there's the – er – vet, if they're ill. And food – yes, food's another thing. You've got to – er – feed them.

D

. . . A dog needs a certain amount of exercise. It's unfair to keep it in the house all day and then to come home and sit yourself down in front of the television all evening. A dog has to have a walk and, if you can, a run about in some kind of open space like a park.

■ Which is the chatty conversation with a friend? Which is the talk to an audience? Give some evidence from the way the extracts are written to show why you decided which was which.

When talking to a friend, you can speak as the ideas come into your head. To talk more formally to an audience needs more thought beforehand.

Tape it

If you have no chance of using a tape or cassette recorder and microphone you should go on to **Prepare a Talk.**

Talking to an audience can be a stressful experience. So can hearing your voice for the first time on tape. With a recorder you can listen critically afterwards to what you have said. It is almost impossible to give a talk and 'listen' to yourself at the same time.

You can use the advice in the next section, **Prepare a talk**, whether you are using a tape recorder or not.

Prepare a talk

You can pick one of the following topics. Or, if you think of a more interesting starting point, you can pick your own topic.

Saturday mornings
An incident on holiday
Preparing a certain kind of food
A television programme
An interesting sport
Jobs about the house
Making something – such as a model or an article of clothing
Your special interest – swimming? CB radio? Snooker? Or something else?

Remember that you are not just chatting. Develop some things to say about your topic. Make some notes. Put them into an interesting order.

At this stage you are not trying to give the perfect talk. You are thinking about the way you sound and trying to improve it.

■ Give your talk. It need not be longer than four minutes. Ask your audience to think about the answers to these questions. (If you are listening to a recording of your talk, you can answer them yourself.)

1 Is the speaker **loud enough**? Can he or she be heard clearly by all the people listening?
2 Is the speaker **speaking clearly**? Does he or she mumble? Does the audience have difficulty in catching some of the words?
3 Is the speaker talking at the **right speed**? Talking to an audience is a strain. It is only human to want to get it over with as quickly as possible. This may make a speaker rush things and talk far too quickly. If a talk has been badly prepared, the speaker may need to pause often to think over what to say next. The right speed will be neither rushed nor fumbling along with many pauses.

Begin your talk

You should plan your talk but don't write it all down and learn it by heart. Try to talk from notes. Start simply and clearly.

■ Here are the opening sentences of two talks. They are both on the same subject. Read them and answer the questions.

E

There are all kinds of fishing. You can catch shrimps sometimes with a net on the seashore. People go fishing for whales. You can go fishing for tadpoles with a jam jar. Not long ago there was a television advert about a man catching a huge marlin – which is a large tropical fish. In some places you can go spear fishing.

F

My talk is about river fishing. My uncle was always a keen fisherman. He used to take me along with him when I was still quite young. That began my interest in river fishing and, as soon as I was old enough to hold a rod, I went river fishing, too.

■ Which of the above passages tells you exactly what the talk is going to be about? Which suggests that the speaker knows about his subject from personal experience?

A useful beginning to a talk will do two things. It will explain exactly what the talk is to be about. It will also explain why the speaker has chosen his or her subject.

The middle of the talk

■ Here are two extracts from the main parts
of two talks. Read the extracts and answer
the questions.

G

You can get some idea of how to decorate a room from books. Any
library will have a shelf of books about homemaking. One of these will
certainly have hints on house decorating. Some local technical or
further education colleges run do-it-yourself classes and, as part of the
course, they also give instruction on decorating. There are many
magazines, nowadays, too, which concentrate on do-it-yourself activities
and these often contain sections on painting and paper-hanging.

H

Mum was away for the week end and we wanted to paper the back
room. Dad was working split shifts and we – that's me and Jill, my sister
– decided we'd make a start. It wasn't too difficult. Jill pasted the

lengths of paper and I put them up and trimmed them. We got one wall done before Dad got home. Some of the paper was a bit wrinkly but we took him up to show him. We knew something was wrong by the look on his face. 'Don't you two know,' he said, 'that wallpapers have a pattern? You've got to fit each length into the pattern.' We could see at once that he was right. I'd just slapped on one length after another all anyhow. There was no pattern. It was all over the place. So that was a lesson to me. When wall-papering, fit each length carefully into the general pattern.

1 Which of the speakers is talking about personal experience?
2 Which might have taken the material for the talk out of a book?
3 Which is more like a list?
4 Which tells a kind of small story?
5 Which of the speakers would you say 'knows' more about the subject?
6 Which speaker seems to have chosen the subject because it is of real interest to him or her?
7 Which speaker seems to have chosen the subject because he or she had to give a talk?
8 Which of the talks do you think you would find more interesting to listen to?

A successful talk will start from a real personal interest in a subject and could be based on personal experience. Use an anecdote – a short account of something that happened to you – to make a talk more interesting.

End a talk

■ Which of these is the end of a talk?

I

There's a lot more I could say about my weekend job. I hope I've said enough though to show you why – most of the time – I like it. Thank you for listening.

J

It gets crowded sometimes late on in the afternoon and I don't like the rush then. Most of the time it's interesting. I don't like it when there's no one in and you just have to stand about.

The answer is that they are both endings. The first one, however, tells whoever is listening that the speaker has finished talking. It is a clear, clean ending. When you finish the talk, make that clear by summing up what you have been talking about or thanking the audience for the attention.

Some more ideas for talks

Do you like doing things on your own? Are you interested in:

motor-cycling music fashion cooking
CB radio fishing photography
collecting things making models reading
making clothes computers swimming pets?

Or do you like being in a group? Are you interested in:

team games football netball tennis
badminton watching motor sport walking
in a group mountain climbing orienteering
judo or any other of the martial arts
belonging to a club dancing?

The media
Television, films and pop music capture the interest of many people. Think of a new approach for a talk on any aspect of these which would give you a starting point.
Is there a pop star or sporting celebrity who interests you?
Is there an interest you follow up by reading a magazine or books?

General
Have you been on an unusual holiday?
Is there a job you do which interests you apart from the money you earn?
Can you maintain a bike or motor-bike?
Decorate a room? Make a child's toy?
Have you some skill at and interest in any do-it-yourself activity?

Spotlight on skills

☆ ☆ ☆ ☆ ☆ ☆ ☆ ☆ ☆ ☆

More on capitals

■ When you write the names of places of entertainment or sports events or teams of players, you begin with a capital. Write these out, putting in capitals where necessary.

1 In our town the regal and the granada used to be cinemas but are now used as bingo halls.
2 In london concerts are usually held in the albert hall while operas are put on at covent garden.
3 The grand national and the derby are probably the two best known horse races in britain.
4 In the south, when you think of cricket, it's lord's or the oval; in the north two well-known grounds are headingley or old trafford.
5 The obvious place to build the royal shakespeare memorial theatre was stratford-on-avon.
6 Do you know where the next olympics will be held?
7 The davis cup is awarded for lawn tennis.

■ The names for special groups of things such as shops, brand names, the names of cars, aeroplanes and other forms of transport are written with a capital letter. Write these out, putting in the missing capitals.

1 In the main street you will find boots, fine fare, woolworths and the halifax building society.
2 After eating oxo, marmite, some rice crispies, a mars bar and half a pound of smarties, he felt he needed a rennie.
3 The sierra and the cavalier are less expensive than an audi or a porsche.
4 At the airshow there were aircraft old and new such as a spitfire, a hurricane, tornados and phantoms.
5 Motor-bikes such as the honda, kawasaki and suzuki ranges are sold all over the world.

■ Names connected with information and entertainment are written with a capital. Newspapers, the titles of books, films, television programmes, plays, pop songs and pop groups are all names that start with a capital letter. Write out the following, putting in the capitals.

1 People who read the times or the daily telegraph don't usually read the dandy or the beano as well.
2 Some of charles dickens' books such as dombey and son and bleak house have been serialised on television.
3 Films that have been great financial successes have been (put in three films).
4 Of all the soap operas on television, coronation street has been the longest-running while dallas has probably been the one most talked about.
5 Those who have never seen it can still tell you that shakespeare's most well-known play is hamlet.

Complete this sentence:
6 At the moment, two groups which are widely known are ....

Complete this sentence:
7 If I were asked which were the two most memorable pop songs I have ever heard, I would name ....

NB: Titles of books, plays and films go inside inverted commas, e.g. 'Treasure Island'.

Communication

Reporting

■ Read the following. Look at the suggestions for the sort of notes to be made and then write out the notes for a report.

Was it a lion?

(Ken and Jill Long are on a caravanning holiday in the West Country. They are being interviewed about a strange animal they saw that morning.)

Ken Long	We were making for Okehampton but we'd parked the caravan just for an overnight stay in this farmer's field near Stenton Gorge.
Jill Long	It was getting dark when we arrived. We didn't see anything then.
Ken	No. And I didn't hear anything strange last night either, did you?
Jill	No. I slept very well. But it was next morning . . .
Ken	Yes. I'd been for some milk. The farm's about half a mile away down a dirt road. I was coming back with the milk and I was in the field . . . . But you saw it first, didn't you, Jill?
Jill	Mm. I was getting our breakfast ready. I looked out of the window and there it was. I just stared at first. I was so surprised. Then I called out to Ken.
Ken	I didn't know what she wanted. I didn't answer her right then. I simply kept on walking. Then, when I got near the caravan, I saw it, too.
Jill	The field was at the edge of a wood. It was in the wood among the trees and grass and brambles and things.
Ken	I thought at first it was a fox. But then I saw that it was too light brown in colour to be a fox.
Jill	And it was much larger than any fox. It was about the size of a Labrador dog.
Ken	Oh, it was far larger than any Labrador, Jill.
Interviewer	Could it possibly have been a very large dog?
Ken	No. Its paws were wrong for a dog. More like a cat's paws but much larger, of course.
Jill	And its head was like a cat's head.

Ken	Yes. Definitely a cat. Not a pet cat, of course — more like a lioness or a tiger.
Jill	It couldn't have been a tiger. It didn't have any stripes. And I thought more of a mountain lion — you know — a puma.
Interviewer	What happened then?
Ken	Well, I was too shocked in that first second to do anything. Then I started to be scared. I shouted something like 'Jill! Jill! Are you all right?'
Jill	Then it hit me that Ken could be in danger. After all, he was outside with the thing. I shouted to him to be careful, to get inside the caravan as quickly as he could. I knocked on the window.
Ken	The lion or puma or whatever it was made a sudden move. That made me jump, too. But then it turned away, back into the wood. It seemed to flow away and vanish. I got inside the caravan as quickly as I could.
Jill	We both sat there sort of shaking a bit. Then we got our nerve back.
Ken	We had breakfast keeping a good look out. Finally, after about an hour, I suppose, I went down the lane to the farm again, told the farmer and he rang the police.

Making basic notes

The sort of questions you might ask yourself before writing a brief report on the passage might be like these. You wouldn't write the questions. But you would write the answers in the form of notes.

What were the names of the two people who saw the animal?
Where were they at the time and what were they doing there?
Where was the animal and about how long did it stay there?
What was its colour?
About how large was it and what did the two people think it was?
What made it finally leave?

■ When you have made your basic notes, you might like to look at the passage again and add any other details or points you think have been missed. Make a note of these. Then write up your brief report from the notes. Use no more than 150 words. Write in paragraphs.

Accident report

On August 18th, the Shastris and their friends, the Freemans went for a day by the sea. Mr and Mrs Shastri were in one car with their two children, Kapil, sixteen, and Alnaz, aged fourteen. The Freemans also had their children with them – Ken, aged twelve, and Lynn, a ten-year-old.

They arrived at Fairthorpe which has a long beach and a wide bay. Mr and Mrs Shastri went for a walk with Mr and Mrs Freeman. The four children blew up an inflatable dinghy that Kapil had brought with him and went out in the bay. It was a bright day but with some wind. Kapil decided to take them out away from the beach where waves were breaking to see if they could find a calmer stretch further out.

Here is a time table of what happened next.

1.30 (approximately) Kapil, Alnaz, Ken and Lynn set off from shore in the dinghy.
1.50 Wind strengthens considerably. Trying to row back very difficult. An oar is lost. Dinghy begins to be blown out to sea.
2.30 Mr and Mrs Shastri and Mr and Mrs Freeman, returning from walk see no sign of dinghy. Short search. Discussion. Very worried. Phone coastguard.
2.35 Lifeboat alerted.
2.30 Ship passing near coast reports probable sighting of dinghy to coastguard. Coastguard passes its position to lifeboat now on search pattern.
3.00 Lifeboat sights dinghy.
3.05 Dinghy picked up. Children cold and frightened but safe and unharmed.

Write the report

You may need to summarise some of the things in the first two paragraphs but you will need to put in names and dates. In the time table, you will probably need to expand the notes – that is to write them out in more detailed sentences.

■ Now write your report in no more than 140 words. Write in paragraphs.

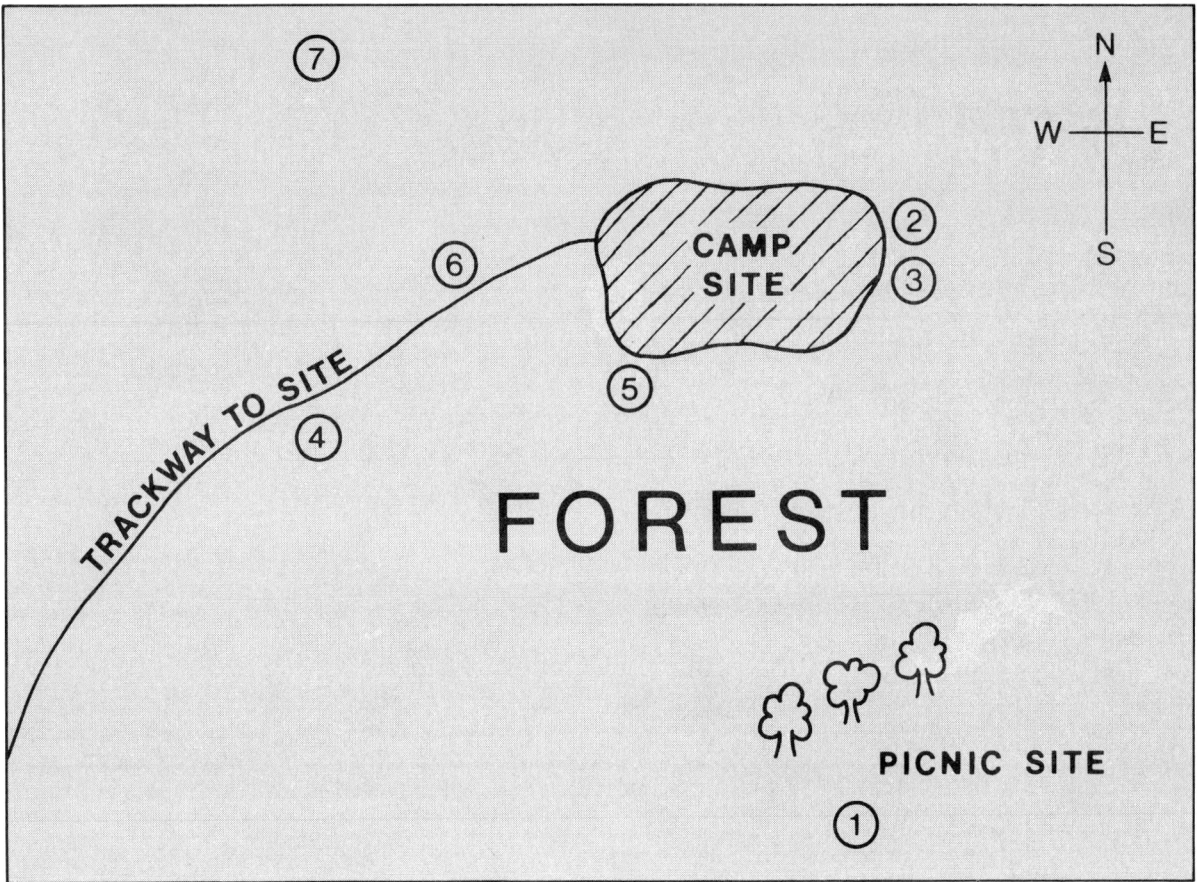

Forest fire

Mr Desmond took his two children, Carol and Wayne camping on a site in Lender Forest. They narrowly escaped being trapped by a forest fire. Above is a map to show the numbered sequence of events.
Here is a key to the numbers.

1 Fire starts here at about 10 o'clock. Emergency services alerted about 10.35. Fire-fighting teams move in. Helicopter on standby.
2 Fire in forest seen here at about 11.00.
3 Mr Desmond and children pack up and move off about 11.20, heading south-west down track.
4 Party stopped here by sighting fire ahead. Decide to return to campsite hoping for chance of rescue there.

5 Fire seen again, raging to east of campsite. Party turns north-west through forest looking for clear path out.
6 Party spotted by helicopter on search.
7 Party picked up here in forest clearing by helicopter.

The fire was eventually brought under control and then an afternoon rainstorm put out what was still burning. It was thought that a cigarette end at the picnic site had started it.

■ Using the information you have been given, write out your report in no more than 140 words. Give your report a title or, if you like, a headline as in a newspaper.

Step 8

In this Step you are shown how to:

■ write a description of someone you know.

■ write in paragraphs.

You are asked to:

■ read about an amazing teacher.

■ discuss a popular song. She's leaving home.

■ conduct a debate.

■ write an article for a magazine and a letter to a newspaper.

Writing

Read this story about an interesting character.

The raffle

They don't pay primary schoolteachers a lot in Trinidad, but they allow
them to beat their pupils as much as they want.

Mr Hinds, my teacher, was a big beater. On the shelf below *The Last
of England* he kept four or five tamarind[1] rods. They are good for
5   beating. They are limber, they sting and they last. There was a tamarind
tree in the schoolyard. In his locker Mr Hinds also kept a leather strap
soaking in the bucket of water every class had in case of fire.

It wouldn't have been so bad if Mr Hinds hadn't been so young and
athletic. At the one school sports I went to, I saw him slip off shining
10   shoes, roll up his trousers neatly to mid-shin and win the Teachers'
Hundred Yards, a cigarette between his lips, his tie flapping smartly over his
shoulder. It was a wine-coloured tie: Mr Hinds was careful about his dress.
That was something else that somehow added to the terror. He wore a
brown suit, a cream shirt and the wine-coloured tie.

15   It was also rumoured that he drank heavily at weekends.

But Mr Hinds had a weak spot. He was poor. We knew he gave those
'private lessons' because he needed the extra money. He gave us
private lessons in the ten-minute morning recess. Every boy paid fifty
cents for that. If a boy didn't pay, he was kept in all the same and
20   flogged until he paid.

We also knew that Mr Hinds had an allotment in Morvant where he
kept some poultry and a few animals.

The other boys sympathised with us – needlessly, Mr Hinds beat us,
but I believe we were all a little proud of him.

25   I say he beat us, but I don't really mean that. For some reason which I
could never understand then and can't now, Mr Hinds never beat me. He
never made me clean the blackboard. He never made me shine his shoes
with the duster. He even called me by my first name, Vidiadhar.

This didn't do me any good with the other boys. At cricket I wasn't
30   allowed to bowl or keep wicket and I always went in at number eleven.
My consolation was that I was spending only two terms at the school
before going on to Queen's Royal College. I didn't want to go to QRC so
much as I wanted to get away from Endeavour (that was the name of the
school). Mr Hind's favour made me feel insecure.

35   At private lessons one morning Mr Hinds announced that he was going
to raffle a goat – a shilling a chance.

He spoke with a straight face and nobody laughed. He made me write
out the names of all the boys in the class on two foolscap sheets. Boys

who wanted to risk a shilling had to put a tick after their names. Before
40   private lessons ended there was a tick after every name.

I became very unpopular. Some boys didn't believe there was a goat.
They all said that if there was a goat, they knew who was going to get it.
I hoped they were right. I had long wanted an animal of my own, and
the idea of getting milk from my own goat attracted me. I had heard that
45   Mannie Ramjohn, Trinidad's champion miler, trained on goat's milk and
nuts.

Next morning I wrote out the names of the boys on slips of paper. Mr Hinds borrowed my cap, put the slips in, took one out, said, 'Vidiadhar, is your goat,' and immediately threw all the slips into the wastepaper basket.

50 At lunch I told my mother, 'I win a goat today.'

'What sort of goat?'

'I don't know. I ain't see it.'

She laughed. She didn't believe in the goat, either. But when she finished she said: 'It would be nice, though.'

55 I was getting not to believe in the goat, too. I was afraid to ask Mr Hinds, but a day or two later he said, 'Vidiadhar, you coming or you ain't coming to get your goat?'

He lived in a tumbledown wooden house in Woodbrook and when I got there I saw him in khaki shorts, vest and blue canvas shoes. He was

60 cleaning his bicycle with a yellow flannel. I was overwhelmed. I had never associated him with such dress and such a menial labour. But his manner was more ironic and dismissing than in the classroom.

He led me to the back of the yard. There *was* a goat. A white one with big horns, tied to a plum tree. The ground around the tree was filthy. The

65 goat looked sullen and sleepy-eyed, as if a little stunned by the smell it had made. Mr Hinds invited me to stroke the goat. I stroked it. He closed his eyes and went on chewing. When I stopped stroking him, he opened his eyes.

Every afternoon at about five an old man drove a donkey-cart through

70 Miguel Street where we lived. The cart was piled with fresh grass tied into neat little bundles, so neat you felt grass wasn't a thing that grew but was made in a factory somewhere. That donkey-cart became important to my mother and me. We were buying five, sometimes six bundles a day, and every bundle cost six cents. The goat didn't change. He still looked sullen

75 and bored. From time to time Mr Hinds asked me with a smile how the goat was getting on, and I said it was getting on fine. But when I asked my mother when we were going to get milk from the goat she told me to stop aggravating her. Then one day she put up a sign:

RAM FOR SERVICE
80 Apply Within For Terms

and got very angry when I asked her to explain it.

The sign made no difference. We bought the neat bundles of grass, the goat ate, and I saw no milk.

And when I got home one lunch-time I saw no goat.

85 'Somebody borrow it,' my mother said. She looked happy.

'When it coming back?'

She shrugged her shoulders.

It came back that afternoon. When I turned the corner into Miguel Street I saw it on the pavement outside our house. A man I didn't know

90 was holding it by a rope and making a big row, gesticulating like anything with his free hand. I knew that sort of man. He wasn't going to let hold of the rope until he had said his piece. A lot of people were looking on through curtains.

'But why all-you want to rob poor people so?' he said, shouting. He

95 turned to his audience behind the curtains. 'Look, all-you, just look at this goat!'

The goat, limitlessly impassive, chewed slowly, its eyes half-closed.

'But how all you people so advantageous? My brother stupid and he ain't know this goat but I know this goat. Everybody in Trinidad who
100 know about goat know this goat, from Icacos to Mayaro to Toco to Chaguaramas,' he said, naming the four corners of Trinidad. 'Is the most uselessest goat in the whole world. And you charge my brother for this goat? Look, you better give me back my brother money, you hear.'

My mother looked hurt and upset. She went inside and came out with
105 some dollar notes. The man took them and handed over the goat.

That evening my mother said, 'Go and tell your Mr Hinds that I don't want this goat here.'

Mr Hinds didn't look surprised. 'Don't want it, eh?' He thought, and passed a well-trimmed thumb-nail over his moustache. 'Look, tell you.
110 Going to buy him back. Five dollars.'

I said, 'He eat more than that in grass alone.'

That didn't surprise him either. 'Say six, then.'

I sold. That, I thought, was the end of that.

One Monday afternoon about a month before the end of my last term I
115 announced to my mother. 'That goat raffling again.'

She becamed alarmed.

At tea on Friday I said casually, 'I win the goat.'

She was expecting it. Before the sun set a man had brought the goat away from Mr Hinds, given my mother some money and taken the goat
120 away.

I hoped Mr Hinds would never ask about the goat. He did, though. Not the next week, but the week after that, just before school broke up.

I didn't know what to say.

But a boy called Knolly, a fast bowler and a favourite victim of Mr Hinds,
125 answered for me. 'What goat?' he whispered loudly. 'That goat kill and eat long time.'

Mr Hinds was suddenly furious. 'Is true, Vidiadhar?'

I didn't nod or say anything. The bell rang and saved me.

At lunch I told my mother, 'I don't want to go back to that school.'
130 She said, 'You must be brave.'

I didn't like the argument, but went.

We had Geography the first period.

'Naipaul,' Mr Hinds said right away, forgetting my first name, 'define a peninsula.'
135 'Peninsula,' I said, 'a piece of land entirely surrounded by water.'

'Good. Come up here.' He went to the locker and took out the soaked leather strap. Then he fell on me. 'You sell my goat?' Cut. 'You kill my goat?' Cut. 'How you so damn ungrateful?' Cut, cut, cut. 'Is the last time you win anything I raffle.'
140 It was the last day I went to that school.

from *The Raffle* in Caribbean Stories by V.S. Naipaul

[1]A tropical tree

Write about Mr Hinds

1 In about 50 words write down how you might recognise Mr Hinds.
2 'He gave us private lessons.' What is unusual about the private lessons?
3 'This didn't do me any good with the other boys.' How did the author suffer by being Mr Hinds' favourite?
4 'Before private lessons ended there was a tick after every name.' Why did the tick show? What did the full list of ticks show about Mr Hinds?
5 'She didn't believe in the goat either.' What does this show about Mr Hinds' reputation?
6 'You kill my goat. How you so damn ungrateful?' Whose goat was it? Explain why Mr Hinds was so angry.
7 'Is the last time you win anything I raffle.' What does this show about Mr Hinds' raffles?

Think again about Mr Hinds

In answering the questions you will have confirmed that it is what Mr Hinds says and does, not what he looks like and wears, that make him an interesting character.

Notice that the few descriptive details are made to stick in your mind by the way they are introduced. We know, for instance, that he wears a wine-coloured tie and smokes because the tie is flapping over his shoulder and the cigarette burning in his mouth while he is winning a hundred yards race. These details fit in with his odd character.

Mr Hinds is in many ways an awful teacher. He has favourites, cheats, lies and beats his pupils viciously. But the boy remembers him almost with affection: 'I believe we were all a little proud of him.' Can you account for this?

Write your own description of a person

■ Write a description of a person you know in about 400 words. Simply tell the reader about him or her, as you might tell your family or friends about someone who has made a strong impression on you. Do not write details of clothes or appearance separately. They will occur to you as you tell the story of the person.

Remember that it is your feelings about the person that will make the reader interested in your portrait.

SELF ASSESSMENT

Read your piece again. Make a list, in note form, of the different things that make up your character's description, eg, lazy, untidy etc.

■ Write a description of the person in the picture.

Understanding

Read this Beatles' song.

She's leaving home

Wednesday morning at five o'clock as
the day begins
Silently closing her bedroom door
Leaving the note that she hoped would
5 say more
She goes downstairs to the kitchen
clutching her handkerchief
Quietly turning the backdoor key
Stepping outside she is free.
10 She (We gave her most of our lives)
is leaving (Sacrificed most of our lives)
home (We gave her everything
    money could buy)
She's leaving home after living alone
15 For so many years, Bye, Bye
Father snores as his wife gets into her
dressing gown
Picks up the letter that's lying there
Standing alone at the top of the stairs
20 She breaks down and cries to her husband
Daddy our baby's gone.

Why would she treat us so thoughtlessly
How could she do this to me.
She (We never thought of ourselves)
25 is leaving (Never a thought for ourselves)
home (We struggled hard all
    our lives to get by)
She's leaving home after living alone
For so many years. Bye, Bye
30 Friday morning at nine o'clock she is far
away
Waiting to keep the appointment she
made
Meeting a man from the motor trade.
35 She (What did we do that was wrong)
is having (We didn't know it was wrong)
fun (Fun is the one thing that
    money can't buy)
Something inside that was always denied
40 For so many years. Bye, Bye
She's leaving home bye bye.

1 Which of these statements best describes the poem? Give reasons for your choice.
It is about young people who leave their parents.
It is about a particular girl leaving her parents.
It is about a particular girl, but is also typical of young people leaving their parents. (2)

2 What signs are there that the girl has taken care to leave secretly? (3)

3 What does her leaving secretly show about her relationship with her parents? (1)

4 Choice of words and phrases is particularly important in poetry. Why is 'clutching' used instead of 'holding'? (line 7) (1)

5 How can the girl be 'living alone' (line 14) when she has been living with her parents? (2)

6 What does 'baby' (line 21) show about the mother and daughter relationship? (1)

7 Explain what is meant by these phrases:
'Leaving the note that she hoped would say more' (2)
'We gave her most of our lives' (2)
'Something inside that was always denied' (2)

8 The bracketed phrases show the parents' thoughts. Show how their thoughts change during the song. (3)

Oral work

■ Write notes on these points raised by *She's leaving home* before discussing them.

1 What 'sacrifices' do parents make for their children? Are they really 'sacrifices' in the sense that they are denying themselves for their children's good?

2 'Never a thought for ourselves.' Are parents being unselfish or selfish when they give up things for their children?

3 'We gave her everything money could buy.' Why might this be an unkind way to treat children?

4 What is meant by 'Some parents try to live their lives through their children'? What pressures does this put on children?

5 What three pieces of advice would you give parents about their treatment of teenage children?

6 What three pieces of advice would you give teenage children about treatment of parents?

Arrange a debate

Debates, like games, have their own rules. The debate starts with what is called a **motion**. This is a sentence stating clearly what the debate is about. It usually starts, 'This house . . .' or 'This class believes . . .'

This house believes that homework should be abolished.
is better than

This class believes that too much homework is given in schools.

The first motion asks for a definite 'yes' or 'no' approach. The second is less definite and asks for 'maybe' or 'it depends'.

Which is best?

Which of these motions or subjects for debate would make people react more strongly in a 'one-sided' way?

1 This class believes that the lives of all animals are sacred.
2 This class believes that some animals should not be killed.

Remember: for a successful debate the subject should be one which interests as many of the class as possible. It is important to choose a motion about which there is going to be some argument. If all the class agree with the motion, there is no point in having a debate.

Group work

To decide on the motion for a debate the class can be divided into groups. Each group discusses and chooses its own motion to offer to the class. These motions are then read out. Then the motion is decided.

Some ideas for debates

Here are some ideas for discussion. Start with one of them. Then work out a one-sentence motion which is of interest to all.

Our environment
Should we have better laws to protect our environment?
Are people creating dangers for future generations by destroying rain forests?
Are farmers responsible enough in caring for the land?
Do factories put too much pollution into the air, rivers and seas?
Are we sure enough of what we are doing when we use nuclear power?

Treatment of animals
Should animals be used for experiments in laboratories?
Are some species of animals dying out and should something be done to save them?
Is factory farming necessary and is it cruel?
Is it fair to keep animals in zoos?
Is it wrong to hunt animals?

People
Would bringing back the death penalty prevent crime?
Should we punish people with racist attitudes, or educate them?
Should we allow such harmful drugs as tobacco and alcohol to be sold?
Is it necessary or uncivilised to have a high degree of unemployment in a society?
Does our society spend its money on the wrong things, such as war and advertising?
Should doctors have the right to let very ill or very disabled babies die?
Does the West do enough about famine and poverty in the Third World?

Other topics
Is there a strike in the news that people are taking sides about?
Should the authorities give in to terrorists to save lives or not?
Should football hooligans be given harsher penalties?
Do you agree or disagree with some recent changes in your school?

Proposing and seconding

In a debate you need:

A chairperson
A proposer who speaks in favour of the motion.
A first speaker who speaks against the motion.
A seconder who speaks in favour of the motion.
A seconder who speaks against the motion.
Then the chairperson will let you speak one at a time.
You take a vote at the end.

Whether you are in favour of a motion or against it, you should prepare what you are going to say. You will have to give evidence to convice others. The best evidence is a set of facts.

■ Which of these would impress you more about the dangers of nuclear war?

A

The bomb that fell on Hiroshima on August 6th 1945 was one of only $12\frac{1}{2}$ kilotons. That is, it was equal to 12,500 tons of TNT. That was only a small bomb in present day terms. Now, even a medium-sized bomb is a megaton bomb. That has the explosive power of one million tons of TNT.

A nuclear bomb is unlike a normal high-explosive bomb in that a nuclear bomb has more effects. The first is the initial radiation. This, from a one megaton bomb will kill all unprotected human beings in an area of six square miles. The second effect is electromagnetic. This knocks out all electrical equipment over a wide area. The fireball, lasting about ten seconds will cause second-degree burns to unprotected human beings even at the edge of an area of 280 square miles. The blast wave will flatten most buildings within a radius of $4\frac{1}{2}$ miles. Fallout after that can poison an area of over a thousand square miles.

This is to say nothing of the fire storm, the world wide fallout and the damage to the protective ozone layer round the earth which may follow even such a medium-sized nuclear explosion.

B

I think nuclear war is a bad thing because it kills so many people. We have had wars before but we have not had wars in which so many people could be killed all at once. Most of the people who die in such a war will not have wanted the war at all and they will have no shelter or protection against a nuclear bomb.

The explosion of the bomb will be terrible enough but those who are not killed or horribly injured by that explosion will probably die later because of the radiation.

You may **feel** strongly enough about something to argue about it. You will argue more strongly and convincingly if you **know** some of the facts.

Prepare for a debate by reading about the subject. Make notes of important facts and figures. These will make your arguments much more powerful.

Speaking in a debate

Speaking in a debate is like other forms of public speaking. Here is a check list of some things to remember.

1 Prepare your convincing facts and put them in order.
2 Speak loudly enough to be heard.
3 Speak clearly enough and slowly enough for your listeners to take in what you are saying.
4 Look at your audience. If you can, see how they are reacting. If someone looks bored, look at that person, as if speaking directly to him or her, until you have his or her attention again.
5 Don't read. Speak and let your tone of voice convey your interest to your audience.

Spotlight on skills

☆ ☆ ☆ ☆ ☆ ☆ ☆ ☆ ☆ ☆ ☆ ☆

Paragraphs

It is essential to divide writing into sections. This is called paragraphing. Each paragraph will be about one theme or aspect of what you are writing about. Some paragraphs are long, others are short.

It is helpful to look in newspapers to see how they paragraph news reports. Newspapers specialize in the short paragraph to make their news more readable. In stories and descriptive writing you will need longer paragraphs.

Here is a news report. The first two paragraphs have been done for you. How would you paragraph the rest?

A cow caused a great deal of trouble yesterday when it became stuck in mud on a canal bank.

The cow's owner, Mr Fred Thompson of Side Hill, went in to pull it clear and became stuck himself. He was stuck for three hours before he could attract anyone's attention.

■ Now paragraph this:

A tractor owned by neighbouring farmer, Mrs Gladys Hinkle, attempted to pull them both clear but itself became stuck. It sank in up to the axles of the back wheels. Finally the Fire Brigade was called and it managed to haul the cow, Mr Thompson and the tractor to safety. 'I began to get a bit worried,' said Fred. 'It was getting dark before I could attract Mrs Hinkle's attention.' Appropriately the cow is called 'Mudlark' as she likes to cool her feet in mud on hot days. 'She will not go in that field again,' said Mr Thompson.

■ Now write part of this as a story. Describe the field, canal etc. Mr Thompson working and finally seeing the cow, his thoughts and feelings as he gets stuck and it begins to get dark. Use longer paragraphs than the news report. You could include:

The field and weather
Description of the canal and mud
Mudlark getting stuck
Mr Thompson mending a gate hears moos of alarm, and so on . . .

What Gear do I need?

Keep it simple is the best advice. Like all pastimes rambling has specialist equipment. You will find a bewildering variety in the outdoor shops. But the essentials are just common sense:

□ Stout shoes or boots, because they support the ankles on rough going and keep out the wet;

□ In winter a thick pullover or windproof to keep you warm and – at all times of the year – a waterproof;

□ For carrying extra layers and lunch, a rucksack, a mini one for a day's outing or a backpacker's full-size job according to need;

□ A stick – optional but handy against nettles, brambles and over-inquisitive livestock;

□ A compass which is a must in the hills – but if you are going off the beaten track you need to know the safety drill: iron rations, competence with compass and maps are vital.

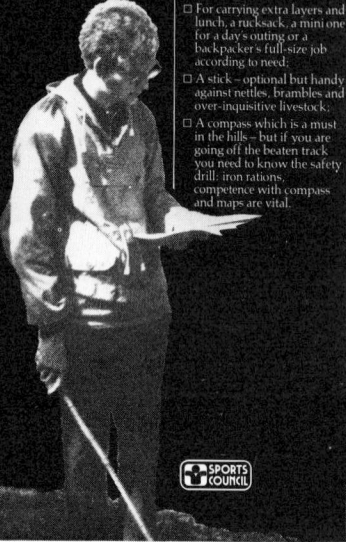

The Ramblers' Association

The Ramblers' Association, the national organisation for all who enjoy walking in the countryside has produced this leaflet in conjunction with the Sports Council to provide basic information to enable you to start rambling.

If you would like to start by walking with a group, the RA has a network of over 220 local Groups which organise programmes of rambles and other activities. In addition, membership of the RA entitles you to a free copy of the Bed and Breakfast Guide produced annually, the journal *Rucksack* published four times a year, local Area News, use of the 1:50,000 OS map library and special offers on publications.

Further Information

Further details about RA membership and Fact Sheet Service can be obtained by sending an SAE (at least 9'' x 4'') to: The Ramblers' Association, 1/5 Wandsworth Road, London SW8 2LJ.

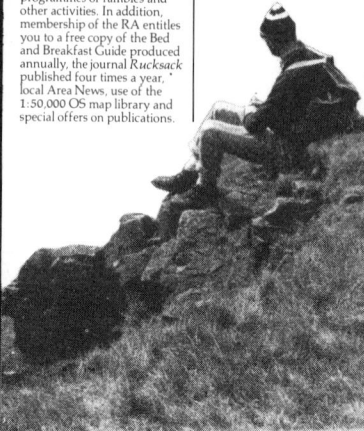

Walking
in the Countryside

Where can I walk?

On the footpaths. More than 100,000 miles of public footpaths and bridleways – both open to walkers – make spiders' webs of beauty and adventure across the countryside. Look for the red dots and dashes on the Ordnance Survey Landranger maps.

On long-distance the long trails. Ten of them are designated and organised by the Countryside Commission. The Pennine Way was the first and the Wolds Way is the latest (1982). But there are also many unofficial routes planned and mapped by ramblers, amenity societies and local authorities. The Oxfordshire Way and the West Midland Way are examples.

On commons, ranging from the gorse-clad heaths of the home counties to the wide pastures of moor and fell in the Pennines, Lake District, Wales and Dartmoor.

On access land, countryside where formal agreements between local authorities and landowners give you the right to wander freely. Such agreements are rare except in the Peak National Park where they cover some 70 square miles. Access land is clearly labelled on site.

On land owned by the **National Trust** and by the **Forestry Commission**. Both these massive landowners normally permit and welcome people on foot. The Commission has many miles of logging tracks as well as laid-out nature trails.

In country parks. You won't be able to do any great distances here; they are intended primarily for people who don't want to go far from the car. But you will be able to stretch your legs and get a lungful of fresh air in some of the bigger ones – for instance Beacon Fell near Preston, Lancs and the Exceat Country Park where the South Downs meets the sea.

Where is the best Country?

England and Wales offer some of the most varied and enchanting landscapes in the world. Most of the very finest are specially protected.

National parks cover some ten per cent of the country and include the best of the wilder countryside in the north, Wales and the south-west. National parks have a duty to promote recreation and you will find information and interpretive centres, guides and leaflets, well-signposted and waymarked paths.

Areas of outstanding natural beauty comprise another ten per cent of the country. As beautiful as the national parks, though generally less rugged, they are more populated and less strictly protected.

Heritage coasts largely overlap with areas of outstanding natural beauty. Many of our finest coast lines are so designated and special attention is given to preventing development and erosion by over-use.

How shall I find the way?

Signposts. Many public paths are signposted where they leave the metalled road; some, but not many, are also waymarked with painted arrows at tricky points.

Maps. Britain is one of the best-mapped countries in the world. The Ordnance Survey, the official survey and mapping agency, covers the whole country with maps of various scales. For walkers the best are the Landranger series at 1:50,000 (about one and a quarter inches to a mile) and the Pathfinder and Outdoor Leisure series at 1:25,000 (about two and a half inches to the mile). The bigger scale of course give you more detail (field boundaries especially) but you can quickly run out of map. The Landrangers won't help when you need to know which side of the fence the right of way is, but they will see you through most walking and give you a good over-view of a decent chunk of country. All these sheets mark rights of way, but the Pathfinder and Outdoor Leisure ones do not yet cover the whole country.

Guidebooks make handy supplements to the maps. There are hundreds of them written just for walkers by local enthusiasts who have picked the best walks and the clearest paths. Often these books have handy sketch-maps and they tell what to see or look for along the way. They also grade the walks by distance so that you can pick an easy stroll for the family with small children or something longer and more demanding. The RA's fact sheets list guidebooks county by county.

Communication

Write an article

■ You have to write an article for your school magazine on **Walking in the Countryside**. You obtain the pamphlet on page 108 for information. Space is limited in the magazine. You can do 100 words on **Where can I walk?**
You can do 50 words on **Where is the best country?**
You can do 50 words on **How shall I find the way?**
You can do 50 words on **What gear do I need?**
Finally include the address of the Ramblers' Association

You score marks for not going over 250 words in all plus the address. You score marks for picking out the main points about rambling. You score marks for writing in sentences to make it read like a proper magazine article.

Write a letter

You are rambling in Exshire. You find a marked footpath on your Pathfinder map barred with barbed wire. You climb the barbed wire ripping your anorak and find that the marked footpath has been ploughed up. At the end of that field you find the footpath has been left but there is a bull in the field. The farm is Manor Farm near the village of Deepdale.

■ Write a letter to the Editor of the *Exshire Mail* alerting other walkers to the problem and asking for action by the County Council. Use your home address.

Write a story

Look at **What gear do I need?** again.

■ Now write a story of about 400 words about a group of children of your age who went walking in winter in a National Park and who did not have the right equipment. They are rescued by a mountain rescue team but some are very poorly.

Divide your story into the following sections

1 The meeting to decide where to go. It could be Snowdonia or the Lake District. Look at a map for names.
2 The general business of getting ready, borrowing tents, stoves, etc.
3 The coach ride to the National Park.
4 Setting out on the walk against the advice of a local farmer.
5 Up on the mountain the weather worsens.
6 Lost in a blizzard, injuries and illness.
7 The rescue.

You score marks for:
Writing in sentences.
Using conversation correctly punctuated.
How real you make the story seem.
Good description of mountain scenery.
Good weather description using adjectives.
The tension you get into your story in sections 5 and 6.

SELF ASSESSMENT

Check very carefully to make sure that you have written in sentences. Check also your speech punctuation. Make a list of the words you have used to describe the weather. Are they the best you could have used?

Step 9

In this Step you are shown how to:

■ write Scene 2 of a play.

You are asked to:

■ answer understanding questions on a passage called *Going home*.

■ work out subject option choices for pupils and take a role in the discussion of the choices.

■ check your knowledge of two uses of the comma.

■ design and write an advertisement.

Writing

A play to finish

People will only be interested in the action of a play if they are interested in the characters involved in the action.

The first scene of this play tells you what is about to happen, and also establishes the characters involved.

Getting your own back

Pam   They'll be at the airport by now. Safely out of the way for a week. Let's go and get our records back.

Ann   But we can't just break into a private house.

Pam   We're not breaking in. We're unlocking the door. I know just where the key's hidden. When we were friends with her, I often used to let myself in, make a drink and wait for her.

Ann   But it's still breaking in.

Vicky   At least let's wait till it's dark. We don't want to advertise the fact that we're breaking into her house.

Ann   And it's not her house. It's her parents', isn't it?

Pam   So what? She's stolen our records. We've a right to take them back.

Vicky   Well, she's not actually stolen them. I mean they belonged to the four of us. We all put the same amount in. I think we should leave her a quarter of them.

Pam   Don't be stupid. She's had them all for about three months. We'll take the lot, and any new ones she's got as interest.

Ann   I think we should just ask her for ours back when she comes home.

Pam   Ask her? How can we do that? We're not speaking to her, remember.

Ann   We might get caught.

Pam   Caught doing what? Taking back what's ours anyway?

Vicky   You're just silly, Pam. We've a right to three quarters of the records, but we've no right to break into her house. It's only sensible to minimise the risk of being caught. We'll go when it's dark, and plan exactly where we're going to look beforehand.

Pam   No problem. They'll be in her smelly bedroom. We'll write her a message on her mirror.

Ann   I'm not doing that.

Vicky   Neither is Pam. There's no point. In and out as fast as we can. No sign we've been there, except our property taken back.

Pam   Have it your own way. Only let's get on with it.

Vicky	Not now. We're waiting till it's dark.
Ann	I don't think I can come tonight.
Pam	Why not?
Ann	I think I might have to . . .
Pam	Skulk in your house, wetting yourself with fright. You're coming. Don't make lying excuses.
Vicky	Leave her alone. She'll come. Won't you Ann?
Ann	I suppose so, but . . .
Vicky	Good, that's settled. Nine o'clock at the roundabout.

Write Scene 2 yourself

Now write Scene 2. It should be about the same length as Scene 1. The plot can develop as you wish, but make sure the characters act consistently – behave in the way established in Scene 1. You should have already decided, for instance, who is really the strongest character, who is liable to do something silly and who is liable to avoid doing anything at all.

SELF ASSESSMENT

Act out your finished plays in groups. Who has made the characters behave in the most consistent way?

112

Understanding

Going home

When Phil saw that all the houses in Morley Street had been knocked down, he turned off the main road and drove slowly between the piles of rubble. He stopped the car and got out but he wasn't sure whether he was where the house had stood or not. All the familiar landmarks had disappeared: lamp posts, corner shops and the covered entries which had punctuated the terraces. The street seemed wider now that all the houses had been demolished. It was lighter too, like a room with the curtains and the furniture removed.

Phil stood there, trying to reconstruct the street which he had grown up in. He remembered all the families who had lived there and, as he scanned the heaps of sooty bricks, he found it difficult to believe that so many people had lived in such a small place.

'Thank God for progress,' he said, as he got back into his car and returned to the main road to continue his journey home.

Phil thought about his mother as he drove down Linnet Close. He imagined her sitting beside him looking out approvingly at the modern detached houses and dormer bungalows, the neat front gardens and caravans on the drives. She would have been proud of him. 'You've come a long way

from Morley Street,' she would have said. Phil would have agreed with her.

He had to drive carefully as he turned in through the gateway. The narrow drive was his only serious criticism of the house. His friends on the road agreed with him. They were always grumbling about their wives scraping their cars against the gateposts on their way in and out.

Phil stood by the car and inspected the front lawn: he had been troubled with worm casts recently. No more had appeared since he went to work, so he plucked all the dead heads off a rose bush and went into the house.

from *Going Home* by Barry Hines

■ Answer the following questions, which test your understanding of the passage.

1 Which street did Phil visit? (1)
2 What was he unsure about when he got out of the car? (1)
3 In what road did Phil live? (1)
4 What, in his mind, was the main drawback about his house? (1)
5 What did he do just before he went inside it? (1)
6 Which single word in the first paragraph means, 'to be inserted into at intervals, to interrupt'? (2)
7 Which single word in the same paragraph means 'completely pulled down'? (1)
8 In your own words explain what the word 'reconstruct' in the second paragraph means in the passage. (2)
9 From what evidence in the passage can you be certain that Phil used to live in Morley Street? (2)
10 What suggests that it was a street where many people lived, crowded into a small space? (2)
11 How can you be fairly sure that Phil has few regrets about having left Morley Street? (3)
12 What seems to indicate that his mother is no longer alive? (2)
13 How do you know that Phil is a fairly careful man who likes things neat and tidy? (2)

Oral work

Here is the type of subject option form most pupils are faced with at the end of their third year. Compulsory subjects, not included in the option form, are Maths, English and P.E. The pupils can pick one subject from each option.

OPTION FORM

Option A	Option B	Option C	Options D	Option E
French	Biology	Geography	Chemistry	Physics
Geography	Geography	Physics	History	Home Economics
History	German	Chemistry	Geography	Biology
Human Biology	Technical Drawing	Drama	Art	Art
	Computer Studies	Art	Craft, Design and Technology	Geography
	Economics	Latin	Computer Studies	Typing
	French	Pottery	Agricultural Sci.	Music
		Woodwork		
		Craft, Design and Technology		
		Home Economics		
		Religious Ed.		

Work out your options

■ Carol wants to take French, Human Biology, Chemistry, Computer Studies and Art. Which options would she choose for which subjects? Work out how she can do this. Under which options must she choose which subjects for the combination to work?

■ Ramin wants to take Drama, Craft, Design and Technology, Geography, Biology and French. Can he do this? Write out his option courses.

■ Mandy wants to take Religious Education, French, Geography, History and Latin. What is her problem?

Role play – a meeting

The pupils' choices have produced difficulties. In Option C only 11 pupils have chosen Drama and only 9 have chosen Latin. 35 have chosen Geography and 38 have chosen Art. It is possible to split the pupils in geography and Art into two groups, but only if the Drama and Latin groups are cancelled, and the pupils asked to choose another subject in the option. The Head Teacher has called a meeting to decide what to do. The people who are present at the meeting are described on pages 116 and 117.

The Head Teacher

The Deputy Head

Head of Geography

Drama Teacher

Latin Teacher

Head of Art

116

The Head Teacher
She will open the meeting by explaining the problem and asking each person for his or her opinion. She thinks that the 38 Art pupils should be split into two groups, and that the Geography class should be 35. This means that only one of the smaller groups will have to be cancelled. She favours keeping the Latin group, because she thinks it is more important than Drama, and that the parents will be impressed by a school prospectus that offers Latin.

The person playing the part of the Head Teacher must be careful how she expresses these views. To do it bluntly might offend two people (which two?). The Head Teacher will probably listen to others' views before she tells her own.

The Deputy Head
He has interviewed all the pupils about their option choices. He has tried to persuade some pupils to take Latin or Drama instead of Geography or Art to balance the groups but so far he hasn't been successful. He is willing to try again if necessary but without much hope of success. He has already been seen by several parents who particularly want their children to take Latin or Drama. One parent who wants his daughter to take Latin is a governor of the school.

Head of Geography
He has become angry over recent years because Geography classes have become steadily larger. He doesn't see why Geographers should have to teach large classes when teachers of subjects like Drama and Latin have such small groups. He thinks that any subject that doesn't have 20 volunteers should be cancelled. This would mean more Geography groups with fewer pupils in each.

Drama Teacher
She has been trying to build a Drama course for several years and feels that if it does not take place this year it will mean the end of Drama as a subject in the fourth and fifth years. She believes that Drama offers qualities that no other subject does, developing self-confidence, speech and understanding of others. Drama is a contrast to the academic subjects.

Latin Teacher
If the Latin course is cancelled, she will have to teach History, a subject she dislikes. She thinks that Latin is one of the few subjects that develop powers of analysis and thought. She thinks that Drama is a waste of time.

Head of Art
He doesn't mind large classes, as long as they can fit into the room. He thinks that the Art department needs more money to buy materials and that smaller subjects are being given too much. He thinks Drama is important and that Latin is a pointless subject.

Divide into groups of six, choose your characters and spend some time individually preparing your arguments.

■ Now hold the meeting. In the end the Head Teacher will have to made a decision. You could appoint someone to act as secretary and record the important points.

Your point of view

■ Write a half-page report on the meeting from the point of view of the character you have been playing. Compare your reports with others.

Further role play

■ A parent (or parents) arrive to see the Deputy Head. They are angry that their son/daughter cannot do the subjects he or she wishes – Music and Typing. Role play the scene in pairs or fours (there could be two parents and their son or daughter).

The parents either do not understand the option system or want it changed. They think that typing is a most important skill and their child is very good at music. The Deputy Head might eventually make some suggestion that the typing could be done after school.

Spotlight on skills

☆ ☆ ☆ ☆ ☆ ☆ ☆ ☆ ☆ ☆ ☆

The comma

Look at these sentences:

Where is the station?
You have done well. Now try another.
This is the playing-field, where the sports are held.

The full-stops and the question mark are definitely needed. The comma is not. You have to decide whether you wish the reader to pause or not. Can you see the difference made to the meaning if you leave out the comma?

Commas are used as invitations for the reader to pause. The writer decides whether a pause would help his or her meaning.

There are two places, though, where commas are definitely needed.

Commas for lists

To separate items in a list.

Example: She was a tall, thin, grey-faced, short-tempered woman. The commas are used to mark off each one of the list of adjectives, except the final one.

Example: They took the dog, the cat, the hamster, the rabbit and the budgie with them in the car.
Note that there is no comma before the 'and'.

■ Write these out, placing the commas correctly.
1 Pots pans opened tins stale loaves milk-bottles and a dirty cloth were scattered about the kitchen.
2 She put antiseptic cream plasters aspirins a pair of scissors and a nasal spray into the medicine box.
3 Shapeless huge grey threatening clouds were looming up overhead.
4 He stacked bread butter tea sugar two tins of beans and a packet of sausages in his trolley.
5 A thin sly jeering smile slowly spread across his face.
6 They needed to buy a cooker two chairs a table a carpet and a bed to furnish the place.
7 The long empty dusty endless road stretched before her.
8 Typewriters calculators paper envelopes and a filing cabinet were neatly arranged in the shop window.

Commas in pairs

Commas may be used in pairs, like brackets, to mark off extra information inserted into a sentence.
Example: Madam Curie, a French scientist, discovered radium.

■ Use pairs of commas to bracket off phrases in these:

1 Geoff Watson the opening batsman scored a century.
2 The trees in the park now bare of leaves stretched skeleton arms to the sky.
3 She told Jayne Willis her best friend about her troubles.
4 Their car a battered old model pulled into the car park.
5 The street lamps dim yellow blobs in the fog threw hardly any light on the path.

Communication

This is part of an advertisement that appeared in the *Radio Times*. The language used in it is called *advertising copy*. Study the advert and then answer the questions on page 120.

If you want to feel full of beans, head for Boots. Because we're making it much easier for people to eat a healthier diet.

We're opening healthy eating Foodcentres in all our larger stores.

And you'll find they're packed full of all sorts of things that are good for you, as well as good to eat.

Beans means protein.

There's an astonishing amount of protein and fibre in beans, with hardly any fat. So we have lots of them.

Haricot beans, mung beans, butter beans, kidney beans, black-eyed beans and borlotti beans, to name but a few.

And since they're not the sort of beans that should end up on toast, there are several recipe suggestions on the labels.

Fast food for vegetarians?

We've also bridged the gap between convenience foods and vegetarian meals.

By introducing a new range of tasty vegetarian dishes that are quick and easy to prepare.

They include Country Casserole, Vegetable Curry, Lasagne, Risotto and Ratatouille.

What they don't include, apart from meat of course, is artificial colours, flavourings or preservatives.

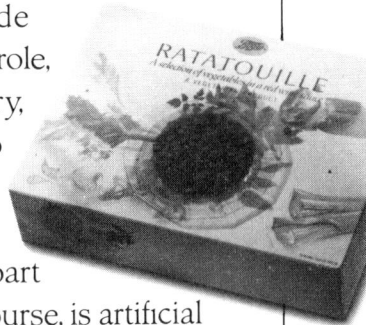

Boots the baker?

There's also a complete range of wholemeal bakery products, bread, scones, even wholemeal doughnuts.

Not to mention fruit juices, cereals, honey, herbs and spices. Plus healthy snacks, vegetable oils and a whole lot more. Pop in and take a look for yourself, if you know what's good for you.

Boots FOODCENTRE

1 Who is the advert aimed at?
2 What habits in people is it trying to change?
3 The large heading said: 'Pop into Boots and check our pulses'. Explain this.
4 Some of the best brains in the country devise adverts. In what ways is this one skilled?
5 Why are the words 'you' and 'yourself' used?
6 Pick out what you think are key words in the advertisement.
7 What do you gather from the advert makes a healthy diet?
8 What would you gather doesn't make a healthy diet?
9 Would this advert influence you in any way at all? Give it a mark out of ten for how much it makes you think about diet.
10 Write a shortened version of it for a TV advert. Use no more than 75 words.
11 Discuss how adverts work.

Make your own advert and advertising copy

Do one of these. The copy is more important than any pictures you draw.

Everyone wants to be healthy. Think of sentences and key words that will persuade them in your advert.

1 Stop pupils in your school from eating too many chips and crisps and to change them to eating something healthier.
2 Persuade people to become vegetarians.
3 Market a new health drink which claims to improve teenage skin.

Step 10

In this Step you are shown how to:

■ write about a family.

■ compare two different kinds of poems about Pigs.

You are asked to:

■ take a role in the organising of a project to raise money.

■ use the apostrophe to show omission.

■ write a letter of application or complaint.

Writing

Write about a family

Your own family and relations may be a very good source of material for writing. Many professional authors write at great length about family experiences.

Here is a piece from a book about South Africa. The mother is forced to work away from home and the family are looked after by a grandmother.

Journey to Jo'burg

Naledi and Tiro were worried. Their baby sister Dineo was ill, very ill. For three days now, Nono, their granny, had been trying to cool her fever with damp cloths placed on her little head and body. Mmangwane,[1] their aunty, made her take sips of water, but still their sister lay hot and
5   restless, crying softly at times.

'Can't we take Dineo to hospital?' Naledi begged, but Nono said Dineo was much too sick to be carried that far. The only hospital was many miles away, and Naledi also knew they had no money to pay a doctor to visit them. No one in the village had that much money.
10   'If only Mma[2] was here.' Naledi wished over and over as she and Tiro walked down to the village tap with their empty buckets. She clutched tightly the coins in her hand.

Each morning the children had to pass the place of graves on their way to buy the day's water and only last week another baby in the village had
15   died. It was always scary seeing the little graves, but especially this fresh one now.

As they came nearer, Naledi fixed her eyes on the ground ahead, trying not to think. But it was no use. She just couldn't stop herself thinking of her own little sister being lowered into a hole in the ground.

20   Finally Naledi could stand it no longer. When they had returned with the water, she called Tiro to the back of the house and spoke bluntly.

'We must get Mma, or Dineo is going to die!'

'But how?' Tiro was bewildered.

Their mother worked and lived in Johannesburg, more than 300
25   kilometres away.

'We can get to the big road and walk,' Naledi replied calmly.

It was school holidays now, but in term time it took the children more than an hour to walk to school each day, so they were used to walking. Naledi wasn't going to let herself think how much longer it would take to
30   get to Johannesburg.

However, Tiro was not so sure.

'But Nono doesn't want us to worry Mma and I know she won't let us go!'

'That's just it,' Naledi retorted quickly. 'Nono and Mmangwane keep
35 saying Dineo will get better soon. You heard them talking last night. They
say they don't want to send Mma a telegram and frighten her. But what if
they wait and it's too late?'

Tiro thought for a moment.

'Can't we send Mma a telegram?'

40 'How can we if we haven't the money? And if we borrow some, Nono
will hear about it and be very cross with us.'

It was clear that Naledi had made up her mind – and Tiro knew his
sister. She was four years older than him, already thirteen, and once she
had decided something, that was that.

45 So Tiro gave up reasoning.

The children went to find Naledi's friend, Poleng, and explained. Poleng
was very surprised but agreed to help. She would tell Nono once the
children had gone and she also promised to help their granny, bringing
the water and doing other jobs.

50 'How will you eat on the way?' Poleng asked.
Tiro looked worried, but Naledi was confident.
'Oh, we'll find something.'
Poleng told them to wait and ran into her house, returning soon with a couple of sweet potatoes and a bottle of water. The children thanked her.
55 She was indeed a good friend.

from *Journey to Jo'Burg* by Beverley Naidoo

1 'little mother'
2 'mother'

■ Write the answer to these questions:

1 What evidence of love and caring is in the passage?
2 What evidence is there that Dineo's life is in danger?
3 What evidence of poverty is in the passage?
4 Why do the children need their mother?
5 In this short extract what characterization is already revealed?

■ Write one of these in about 400 words. It could be about your family or it could be a made-up family.

1 'I shall never forget the day the neighbours moved in.'
2 'It all started with the baby crying . . .'
3 How we get on with our relations.
4 The day we moved house.
5 'As I lay in bed I heard the door slam and I knew she (or he) had gone . . .'
6 The family celebration that was a great success, or the family party that went wrong.
7 The day we had to make a big decision.
8 What happened after grandma (or grandad) moved in.

Think about these things in your writing about families:

good character descriptions
some description of home
things that irritate people
family love or lack of it
habits of people, particularly those that irritate
actual things your family say – any favourite expressions
the part friends and neighbours play
the strengths and weaknesses of your family

You may like to discuss in small groups before you begin your writing.

SELF ASSESSMENT

Compare your piece with a neighbour. Whose sounds the most like a real family? Who has put in the oddest or most unusual things?

Understanding

Read these two poems about pigs.

A – View of a Pig

The pig lay on a barrow dead.
It weighed, they said, as much as three men.
Its eyes closed, pink white eyelashes.
Its trotters stuck straight out.

Such weight and thick pink bulk
Set in death seemed not just dead.
It was less than lifeless, further off.
It was like a sack of wheat.

I thumped it without feeling remorse.
One feels guilty insulting the dead,
Walking on graves. But this pig
Did not seem able to accuse.

It was too dead. Just so much
A poundage of lard and pork.
Its last dignity had entirely gone.
It was not a figure of fun.

Too dead now to pity.
To remember its life, din, stronghold
Of earthly pleasure as it had been,
Seemed a false effort, and off the point.

Too deadly factual. Its weight
Oppressed me – how could it be moved?
And the trouble of cutting it up!
The gash in its throat was shocking, but not pathetic.

Once I ran at a fair in the noise
To catch a greased piglet
That was faster and nimbler than a cat,
Its squeal was the rending of metal.

Pigs must have hot blood, they feel like ovens.
Their bite is worse than a horse's –
They chop a half-moon clean out.
They eat cinders, dead cats.

Distinctions and admirations such
As this one was long finished with.
I stared at it a long time. They were going to scald it,
Scald it and scour it like a doorstep.

Ted Hughes

B – The Irish Pig

'Twas an evening in November,
As I very well remember,
I was strolling down the street in drunken pride,
But my knees were all aflutter
So I landed in the gutter,
And a pig came up and lay down by my side.

Yes, I lay there in the gutter
Thinking thoughts I could not utter,
When a colleen passing by did softly say,
'Ye can tell a man that boozes
By the company he chooses.' –
At that, the pig got up and walked away!

Anonymous

■ Answer the following questions about the two poems.

Poem A

1 'It was less than lifeless, further off.'
   What does 'further off' mean? (2)
   This line is the poet's main thought about the pig. How does he illustrate it by two comparisons? (2)

2 Which of these feelings did the dead pig arouse in the poet? Explain why it didn't arouse the others.
   guilt
   laughter (4)
   shock
   sympathy

3 The dead pig reminds the author of a live one. What points does the author make about the live pig in the fair? (2)

4 Why does he mention these particular points? (2)

5 Why does the poet mention that pigs eat cinders and dead cats? (2)

6 In one sentence say what you think is the main point of the poem. (4)

Poem B

1 How is the man's drunkenness shown? (2)
2 What double significance has the title? (2)
3 Is the poet making a serious or comic comment on drunkenness? (3)
4 What is implied by the last line? (2)

Compare the Poems – rhythm

■ Which opening two lines do you read more quickly? Why is a quick rhythm suitable to one poem, and a heavy rhythm suitable for the other?

■ Which are the three heavy sounding syllables in this line?

'A poundage of lard and pork'

■ The next line reads more quickly.

'Its last dignity had entirely gone'

Which vowel sound occurs three times in this line and not at all in the previous one? Write three words from the poem that make a sharp sound because of this vowel.

■ Where does the rhythm in 'View of a Pig' become faster? Why does the poet want to make it faster?

Compare the poems – rhyme

■ Which of these two couplets (two rhyming lines) *sounds* as if it is taken from a comic rather than a serious poem?

Yet let me flap this bug with gilded wings
This painted child of dirt that stinks and stings

Here lies a man who was struck by lightning
He died when his prospects seemed to be brightening

■ Find two rhymes in 'The Irish Pig' that sound comic. What makes them sound so?

Oral work

Raising money

■ Work in groups of five or six. Imagine your school wants to buy a bus. The Local Education Authority has said that if the school raises £2,000 they will pay the rest. Your group has to plan the project. You meet to decide on the best method of raising the money. At the end of the meeting you will write a report and make recommendations to the Head.

Spend ten minutes considering or making notes on these points before the meeting.

1 Do you prefer a sponsored event for the whole school (what type?), a series of events (garden fete, dance, raffle) or a straightforward appeal (to parents or the whole community)?
2 Who would take part in and organise the appeal or events? (For instance, would each form be allowed to decide in what way it should help or should certain sections of the school organise different events?)
3 How would the money be collected? Should there be prizes for pupils making the best contributions?
4 What snags can you foresee? (For instance, bad weather will hamper an outside event.)

You will need a chairperson and a secretary, who will make notes during the meeting. At the end of the meeting each member of the group should write a report, making definite recommendations (with reasons) about the way the money should be raised and the organisation needed.

Spotlight on skills

☆ ☆ ☆ ☆ ☆ ☆ ☆ ☆ ☆ ☆

The apostrophe for omission

It is easy to get the apostrophe in the wrong place. Many adults do in their writing. The apostrophe shows that letters are missing. **Remember** it goes in the place where the letter or letters are missing and not where words join. For example:

don't (do not) – the **o** of **not** has been left out.
can't (can not) – the **no** of **not** has been left out.

They're It's don't can't

■ Put in these apostrophes:

Ill Ive Im hes shes wouldnt couldnt shouldnt weve theyve theyre mightnt youve its theres didnt mustnt darent theyd shed

■ Then write out their full versions without the missing letter or letters, for example I will – I'll

Problems with apostrophes

■ What is the difference between **your** and **you're**?

Give me your book, please.
You're the last one to know.

■ What is the difference between **there**, **their** and **they're**?

There they are.
They lost their place in the queue.
They're looking very wet.

■ What is the difference between **its** and **it's**?

The cat lost its tail.
It's hard to tell the full story.

■ If you write slang or dialect speech in your stories you may want to miss out letters. Translate this piece of Cockney:

'e 'it 'im on the 'ead with a 'ammer.

Does your local dialect leave out any letters?

Communication

A choice of letters

■ Write to the secretary of a local cricket, tennis or other sports club, asking for details of how to become a member, amount of subscription and details of playing or practice times. The secretary is Alison Wadworth. She lives at 5, Coney Terrace, Walton. WN2 4XS.

■ Write a letter of application for this post.

```
JUNIOR CLERK - aged 16-17, for
accounts office. Good salary and
prospects. Apply David Jones,
Personnel Officer, Dixon Mail
Order Company, 11, Fristy Road,
Birmingham, B4 72P.
```

Include details of qualifications you have or hope shortly to have.

■ Write to the BBC, Television Centre, Wood Lane, London, W12 7RJ either complaining about the quality or timing of a programme or congratulating them on some feature you admire.

Use short paragraphs in each letter.

Step 11

In this Step you are shown how to:

■ write a memo.

You are asked to:

■ respond to an article on an island permanently contaminated by an atomic explosion.

■ make judgements on some points of view.

■ discuss bad behaviour in sport.

■ use the apostrophe to show one person ownership.

Writing

Look at the evidence

A friend says to you:

'I'll be all right in the event of a nuclear war. My Dad's going to have a proper shelter built underneath our house.'

You then read this article in a newspaper:

Last farewell to a contaminated island

THE ENTIRE population of the contaminated atoll of Rongalap, their personal belongings, and most of their houses had been ferried by the Greenpeace ship, Rainbow Warrior to a new home yesterday. Now the 320 people can start a new life without the fear that everything they eat contains plutonium and cesium sucked up from the earth, the residue from America's 1954 Bravo bomb set off at Bikini.

The people have hopes that they can soon become self-sufficient rather than live on American handouts. At their new home, Mejato, in the Kawajelin atoll, 100 miles from Rongalap, they face many practical difficulties just to survive. First of all, they have to rebuild their houses, dig new wells and then begin to cultivate the wilderness that is their previously uninhabited island.

Despite these difficulties, there was no question in the minds of the islanders that they should leave Rongalap.

PAUL BROWN, aboard Rainbow Warrior, in the Marshall Islands, on the final, sad flight from US A-bomb fallout

Muvenarik Kebenli, aged 68, had elected to be the last to leave the atoll. Even then, she had only left after a promise from Senator Jeton Anjin that he would bring her body back when she was dead to be buried in the island's tiny graveyard next to her parents.

She was on the island at the time of bombs and remembers the terror of it as the multiple explosions filled the western sky. She remembers the fallout she thought was flour, which turned yellow in water, and turned the palms of her hands black when she touched it. She remembers the sickness that followed, the skin burns, the shock of, everyone's hair falling out.

Since then she has seen the new illnesses among her people, including children, then unborn. The islanders

never experienced them before the tests. At times she has left the island to live with friends. "Although I love this place, I always feel sick when I return," she said.

The Rongalap people had planned to take their pigs and chickens with them to their new home but they were stopped from doing so by the man who gave them their new island home, Kenja Tumler. He said it was wrong to bring contaminated animals and he would give them new stock.

The move has taken 12 days of unceasing work. The ship was loaded four times in Rongalap using Greenpeace inflatables and the village "boom-booms." This is a Marshalese name for any boat with an outboard motor. . . in this case a

communally-owned cabin cruiser.

Unloading took longer than Greenpeace had bargained for. Lines of Marshalese stood waist-deep in the water to pass their belongings over their heads hand to hand to shore. The operation was both hard and dangerous, sometimes continuing despite rough seas. At the end, hardly anyone on board was without an injury, although the biggest bandage was needed for the French TV cameraman who fell out of his bunk.

Glen Alcalay, an anthropologist, who speaks Marshalese, said the struggles of the people were just beginning. "They were used by the Americans as guinea pigs to study the effects of fallout and they still studied." They had become dependent on American aid and now because of their continued sickness, are forced from their homeland for the sake of their children. That is like taking their souls.

■ List five main things you could then say to your friend of what life might be like for those who survive a nuclear war. Remember Britain is a very crowded island compared to this small habitation in the middle of the Pacific Ocean.

Note: Rongalap was 80 miles downwind of the atomic test. It is thought that it will remain contaminated for thousands of years.

Respond to a piece of writing

■ Write in about 100 words a farewell to the island that Muvenarik Kebenli might write.

or

■ Write the letter she might have written to Greenpeace or the US Government asking to be removed from the island to a place of safety.

or

■ Write about your general feelings on the subject of nuclear testing in about 200 words.

SELF ASSESSMENT

When you have finished your piece see if you have used ten nouns or adjectives or more that were in the newspaper passage. Make a list of any new words you have learned.

Understanding

Below are three opinions about various games.

In praise of volleyball

I recommend volleyball as a far more suitable game for schools than cricket and rugby. Volleyball can be played with a high degree of skill, as is shown in the standards reached by teams at the Olympic Games. But it can also be played and enjoyed by those with very little skill. Cricket is misery for the non-athlete. He is never allowed to bowl, his turn with the bat is short, often scorned by the more accomplished, and sometimes dangerous. Rugby is even worse; it is a licence for the non-athletic and nervous to be assaulted by the large, fierce and insensitive.

Volleyball can be enjoyed by both boys and girls. Its rules are easy to understand. Each player is allowed an almost equal turn, and there is no physical danger for those whose interest in games is limited to taking exercise with others in an organised team game.

Judging points of view

■ Complete these sentences.

1 The main aim of the writer is to persuade people that ____ .
2 Volleyball can be a very skilful game but the writer recommends it mainly because ____ .
3 The writer condemns cricket as a game for non-athletic people because ____ .
4 Rugby, the writer says, is even worse than cricket as a school sport because ____ .

Give your opinion

■ In a paragraph of six to eight lines say whether you agree or disagree with the writer. You might consider these points.

1 Are pupils made to play games such as cricket or rugby against their wishes?
2 Do people who can't play these games well really suffer as the writer says?
3 What other sports are there that offer as good a chance of taking part if you are not very athletic?
4 Are there disadvantages in the game of volleyball that the writer hasn't mentioned?

Bad behaviour by sports people

The players of some sports behave much better than the players of others. This is partly a matter of traditional behaviour associated with particular games. A cricketer may show by his expression his disapproval at being, in his opinion, unfairly given out, but I have yet to see one swipe down his stumps in a rage, or menace the umpire with his bat. Such behaviour would be unprecedented, and probably unthinkable.

But the different standards of behaviour in different sports are only partly matters of tradition. Certain games by their very nature are more likely than others to cause disputes. Golfers, for instance, can only blame themselves for their poor play; tennis players, on the other hand, can blame umpires and linesmen. The source of the bad behaviour shown by many tennis players lies in the game's basic weakness. The way to beat your opponent is to place the ball as near to a line as possible without going over it. When the ball travels at speed it is difficult to tell whether it is in or out. Even the 'magic eye' now used at Wimbledon and other tournaments has not solved this problem.

Every dispute in tennis is about the same 'in or out' problem. It is a weakness of the game which, though not excusing bad behaviour, explains why so much unpleasantness exists in the game today.

■ Answer these questions.

1 Explain in your own words as far as possible, the meaning of 'This is partly a matter of traditional behaviour associated with particular games.'

2 What example does the writer give to illustrate this statement?

3 Explain why the writer thinks that golf is not likely to make players behave badly.

4 Why does the writer think that tennis is likely to make players behave badly?

Oral work

Give your opinion

Below are ten opinions, the first two based on the last passage, the others more general. You are allowed ten minutes to think about the opinions.

■ Work in groups of four. Take it in turns to select a person in the group to speak for a minute on the subject you have chosen for him or her. Allow a further minute for the speaker to answer any questions or comments the other three wish to ask.

1 Tennis players behave no worse than other sportsmen. It's the television and newspaper reporters who concentrate on the bad behaviour and not on the game.

2 It is easy to stop tennis players behaving badly. Just ban them from playing for six months. They would soon behave.

3 The driving test is not strict enough. They should test driving at night and on motorways.

4 Sex education lessons are stupid. You get plenty of education of that sort from people your own age.

5 Dog licences should cost £50. That would make sure people really wanted their dogs and wouldn't neglect them.

6 If the country wants to save money, the Government should get rid of all the weather forecasters and replace them with a chap forecasting from studying a piece of seaweed. He couldn't do any worse.

7 Nobody should be made to play games at school. You come to school to learn; you can play games in your own time if you want to.

8 Girls are better than boys at subjects such as English. Boys are better than girls at subjects such as Maths.

9 Do you have to be a certain height to become a policeman or woman? The same should apply to teachers, nowadays.

10 Newspapers are full of lies. The only thing in them you can believe is the date.

Spotlight on skills

☆ ☆ ☆ ☆ ☆ ☆ ☆ ☆ ☆ ☆

The apostrophe for one person ownership

Debbie owns that radio.
Or, to put it another way:
It's **Debbie's** radio.

To show possession or ownership we can use an apostrophe (') and an 's' at the end of a word. **The hat of the man blew off** sounds peculiar. **The man's hat blew off** sounds much more usual.

Kevin's records

Peter's radio

Jane's room

Ali's cat

■ Use the apostrophe and s to complete these.

1 She borrowed one of Kevin __ records.
2 The school __ reputation was at stake.
3 Coming in late, he kicked the dog __ water bowl across the kitchen and woke everyone up.
4 Uncle never did a hand __ turn in the house to help.

■ Write these out in the more usual way.

5 The siren of the ship could be heard for miles.
6 Suddenly the engine of the car choked and died.
7 A cape of a policeman was spread over the injured boy.
8 Early that morning the van of a milkman came rattling down the road.

Communication

Write a memo

A memo (memorandum) is a note used to send messages to employees in a business.
It is usually set out like this.

```
                        MEMO


From      Mr Singh              Date  7.8.86

To        Miss Roberts          Time  9.30

Subject:  I seem to have mislaid the CONTACT file.  Will you please

          check where it might be.  I last had it in Mr Timms' office.


Reply:    It was in Mrs Salmon's office.  She was putting some details

          in the computer.
```

You need to be as careful with the wording of memos as you do with letters. The wrong choice of words could cause problems.

For example, in Step 5 the manager of the Garden Centre which sent the wrong roses to Mrs Wills, said that Bob Parsons hadn't checked the order carefully enough.

■ Imagine you are the manager's secretary, and have been asked to tell Bob to be more careful. Copy out the memo form and use it to send him a reminder. Remember you know him; he works for the same company. Don't be rude, but make sure he knows he must be more careful. Make up details of names and date. When you have finished swap with your neighbour and write Bob Parsons' reply.

■ You are the manager of a hotel. A delegation of sixty business people have booked for the week 11th – 18th October and are using your conference room. Seven are vegetarians. They will take all meals in the hotel and have especially asked for speedy service so that they can spend as much time as possible in their meetings. Write a memo to your chef, telling him/her the details and reminding him/her of how important such conferences are to the hotel.

■ You are the secretary to the manager of a factory making typewriters. The manager asks you to send a memo to all the staff reminding them of the regulations they agreed to limiting tea-breaks to one of twenty minutes in the morning and one of fifteen minutes in the afternoon. Many employees are going early and coming back late. Send the appropriate memo. Remember not all employees are at fault. Try not to offend, but make the manager's feelings clear.

Step 12

In this Step you are shown how to:

■ Express a point of view.

You are asked to:

■ answer questions on *The duck-walk*.
■ discuss changing attitudes to boy/girl relationships.
■ use the apostrophe to show more than one owner.
■ write a persuading letter.

Writing

Express a point of view

■ Write about the changes you would like to see in your school. You might write about the subjects taught (the option chart on page 115 will help remind you what is, or could be available), the rules, buildings, organisation or anything that you wish, except comments on individuals.

This also gives you a chance to emphasise the good aspects, perhaps asking for some subjects to have more time. Give reasons and examples to illustrate your statements.

Before you begin, look at the piece of writing that follows. It contains most of the mistakes that are made when we are asked to write our opinions.

The changes I would like to see in my school.

In this subject there are alot of pionts to think about, there are some things I would change but there are some things that I wouldn't.

I would definately stop assembleys because they are realy boring.
Sometimes parsons come and they tell long boring stories that you can't
5 hear anyway. Father Drury is the only one that is any good. He always
makes it a good laugh.

I think active tutorials are a waste of time. All you do is filling in forms
about yourself. They are not proper lessons at all.

I would change the uniform but not the color, I wouldn't make pupils
10 wear jackets. It would be just as good to have a sweater or T shirt in the
school colors.

You would have to keep subjects like English and Maths and you need
to know Geography and History, I don't agree with French though,
because you only need it if you go to France.

15 There should be more CDT, this will help you later in life.

Another thing is music. The type of music we have is not interesting,
this needs livening up.

Homework should be cut down but not stopped. I think one homework
every night is about all you have time for, especialy if you have a job like
20 working in the market.

If you don't like games they should let you go home instead, if you
have to wait for the bus there should be a place to do your homework.

I would let pupils go down the town at dinner-time, the ones that muck
about should be caught and made to stop in school.

25 If your parents agree with you smoking it should be allowed if your
sixteen but only at dinner time or break in a specail room.

I think that is about all the changes I would make.

Paul (16)

Comments on the writing

1 The opening paragraph states the obvious. The piece would be better without it, starting with the point about assemblies. If you have an introductory paragraph, it should show the reader clearly what your essay will deal with. For example:

> 'There is nothing I object to in the organisation of the school, and I would only make small changes in the rules, but I do think that far too much time is given to certain subjects.'

2 The short paragraphs show the writer is noting points as he thinks of them. There is no organisation; he hasn't grouped similar points together.

3 The conclusion merely shows he has run out of ideas. It should make a summary of what has been written and perhaps add a new thought. For example:

> 'Most of the changes I would make involve my personal likes and dislikes. Other people might not agree with me, but I think that pupils and their parents should have more chance to make their opinions known than they do now, particularly on subjects such as rules and uniform.'

4 The writer's points need illustrating. What, for instance, makes Father Drury's assemblies good? A small illustration would help to show us why the writer thought the others were boring.
It is difficult to believe that active tutorials consist only of formfilling. Even if it were true, however, some examples of the type and purpose of the forms would add interest.

Now begin your piece of writing.

SELF ASSESSMENT

When you have finished your piece count up and see how many arguments you have used. If you have written only a few, rewrite to add a few more.

Understanding

The duck-walk

The polling station was a local school. Straggling past the school, as I went in, were two pairs of teenaged girls and two pairs of teenaged boys.

Each pair independent of the others. Walking, according to sex, in opposite directions.

5 Coming out of the school, I was surprised to see the same two pairs of teenaged girls and the same pairs of teenaged boys.

Still walking in opposite directions. But this time, if you follow me, in OPPOSITE opposite directions.

Clearly, they'd all been to their respective ends of the street, then
10 retraced their steps. But why? They weren't taking a constitutional, because teenagers don't take constitutionals. They weren't waiting for their mums, because they would have regarded themselves as above the mum-waiting age. They weren't demonstrating for votes at fifteen, because they didn't have placards. So what were they up to?

15 Then, as the first pair of girls passed the second pair of boys, I saw two sets of female shoulders shaking in a repressed fit of the giggles. And the penny dropped. What I'd stumbled across was the local duck-walk.

If you don't know what a duck-walk is, have no fear. I am about to tell you more about the subject than you can possibly need to know.

20 A duck-walk is a length of pavement, stretch of recreation ground, boating lake perimeter, park bandstand circumference, shopping parade diameter, or any other form of measured mile give or take a hundred yards or so, where the lads and lasses of the town perambulate in the hope of – to use the phrase of my long-lost youth – getting off with each other.

25 I didn't know the institution still existed. I thought it all happened in youth clubs and discotheques these days.

For the record, the two pairs of teenaged boys outside my polling station successfully got off with the two pairs of teenaged girls. But I'm afraid I can't report to you on the technique employed. I was already
30 back in the world of boogie-woogie, Arthur English ties, milk shakes, Andy Hardy films – and the duck-walk.

There were several duck-walks where I used to live. One in the park, one around the parish church, one in the middle of the bluebell woods for advanced practitioners, and one near the public library. The public
35 library concession was the one favoured by my best friend and me.

Duck-walk etiquette required that you had to have your best friend with you – one of you brilliantined to the eyebrows, the other not. In the case of girls, the rule seemed to be that the one most closely approximating Doris Day should be accompanied by a juvenile Martha Raye, or an old
40 boot as she was colloquially known.

I believe the process is called natural selection.

The main advantage of the duck-walk was that you were able to examine the goods at leisure before you bought them. If you and your best friend didn't fancy Doris Day and Martha Raye, it was like the
45   conductress always used to say when the last tram was full: 'There'll be another along in a minute.'
    You strolled, always in pairs, from north to south or south to north depending on your sex; or, in the case of the boating lake, clockwise or anti-clockwise; or, in the case of the advanced practitioners in the bluebell
50   woods, a zig-zag course ending in screams of terror (I think they were screams of terror) among the deep ferns.
    As for the public library route, the drill was this. Say you're my best friend and I'm me, and Doris Day and Martha Raye are just walking

55　down from the chip shop limits of the duck-walk. Just as they're minneying by with their noses stuck in the air, we make a clicking noise with our tongues, which naturally they ignore.

But we watch them carefully when they've gone by. If one of them gives the other a shove fit to send her into the gutter, it means we've made it. In the vernacular, we've clicked.

60　On with the ritual. They get as far as the public library and retrace their steps. We reach the chip-shop and retrace ours. Thus we meet again, this being a small world. And after a bit of badinage, such as, 'Does your mother know you're out?' or, 'Are there any more at home like you?' to which the witty response might be, 'Get off your knees!' or 'Go on home,

65　your mother wants your boots for loaf tins,' a lifelong friendship lasting at least two weeks is struck up.

Guess who gets Doris Day. And guess who gets the old boot.

Still, they were happy days. And still are, apparently. And I didn't talk about the election, did I?'

70　　　　　　　　　　　　　from the *Daily Mirror* (article by Keith Waterhouse)

■ Answer these questions by writing in sentences:

1　What is a duck-walk?　(2)
2　Why might it be suitably named?　(2)
3　What does 'OPPOSITE opposite directions' mean?　(2)
4　What is a constitutional?　(1)
5　Is a repressed giggle: a) when you try not to laugh, b) when you laugh out loud, c) when you just titter?　(1)
6　Is the writer making fun of teenagers or writing seriously?
　Give one piece of evidence for your answer.　(2)
7　Has the polling station any importance in the story?　(1)
8　Write down four pieces of evidence that could roughly date the age of the writer.　(4)
9　What did the writer think all happened in discotheques and youth clubs?　(2)
10　Perambulate means: a) to push a pram, b) to walk slowly up and down, c) to rush about.　(1)

11　What are 'advanced practitioners'?　(2)
12　Explain duck-walk etiquette as outlined by the author in a short paragraph.　(2)
13　What does 'natural selection' mean? About what is the term normally used?　(2)
14　Explain in your own words what is the main advantage of the duck-walk.　(3)
15　Doris Day and Martha Raye were film stars of the author's boyhood. What is the main difference between them?　(2)
16　Why does the author use a word like 'drill'?　(2)
17　What might 'minneying' mean?　(2)
18　What was the sign that the boys had 'clicked' or 'made it'?　(1)
19　Write down one piece of badinage from the passage.　(1)
20　What is the author being when he says 'a lifelong friendship lasting two weeks'?　(2)

Oral work

Changing customs

Diane wants to go to Corfu with her boyfriend. She is seventeen and has been at work for eight months. She is a shop assistant. She is a very independent girl but the only child in the family.

Mark is her boyfriend and comes from a big family. He has been abroad before and feels he knows the ropes about foreign travel. He is keen to show Corfu to Diane. He loves her very much – perhaps a little more than she loves him.

Diane's Mum thinks that Diane should not go abroad with just Mark. She fears she will get pregnant. She also is not keen on Diane going by plane because of hijackers and bombs. She worries about Diane all the time, never going to sleep until she is in at night.

Diane's Dad can't see why they both can't go to Blackpool with them. He refuses to lend Diane money to go abroad. He has seen Mark, who is 19, in the pub on several occasions, on one of which Mark was drunk. He does not think he is responsible enough to take his girl abroad.

■ Divide into groups of four and each take a role.

■ When you have finished, from memory, script part of the play that comes out of your role play.

Spotlight on skills

☆ ☆ ☆ ☆ ☆ ☆ ☆ ☆ ☆ ☆ ☆ ☆

Apostrophe to show more than one owner

The **cat's** eyes gleamed
The **cats'** eyes gleamed.

What's the difference? The apostrophe after the 's' in the second sentence shows that there are several cats. If a word already ends in 's' because it is in the plural, add only an apostrophe to show possession (mistresses' rooms).

■ Write these out, putting in the apostrophe correctly.

1 The two of them had flooded the boys cloakroom.
2 All the ships crews went ashore together.
3 The sound of the cars engines on the track was deafening.
4 The Smiths holiday was cut short by illness.
5 The girls team won; the boys team didn't.
6 The actresses parts were missing.
7 The waitresses trays were all full.

Communication

Letters to annoy or letters to persuade

Read the two letters opposite.

Which letter succeeds?

■ Answer by putting 'Letter A' or 'Letter B'.

1 Which letter makes threats?
2 Which letter opens with a kind of explanation or apology?
3 Which letter gives the most detail about the actual damage done by the dog?

4 Which letter takes the angriest tone about the damage?
5 Which letter suggests some sensible ways of solving the problem?
6 Which letter seems to suggest that one way to solve the problem is to kill the dog?
7 Which letter is most insulting?
8 Which letter has the friendliest and most reasonable tone?
9 If you were Mr Watson and fond of your dog, which letter would you find most annoying?
10 If you were Mr Watson and a reasonable man, which letter would make you want to do something about the problem?

Write your own persuading letters

■ Imagine that you have found yourself in the following situations. Your letters should be polite but firm.

1 Someone you know but find boring has taken it for granted that you will go away on holiday together. Write a letter to him or her saying that you can't go.
2 You have stayed at a hotel on holiday. The food was bad and the staff were not polite. You could invent other reasons why the holiday was not a success. Write a letter to the manager or the Head Office of the company that owns the hotel explaining why you thought the holiday was far too expensive under the circumstances and asking them what they intend to do about it.
3 You are a parent. You have a son or daughter who has been rowdy at school. The school is going on a trip to see something that your child is very interested in. Because of rowdiness, he or she has been banned by the headmaster from going on the trip. Write a letter to the Head asking that your child be allowed to go. You could give your personal assurance that he or she wouldn't misbehave on the trip. You could suggest some alternative punishment, if your child is allowed to go.

144

Letter A

4 Norton Drive
Weston

June 4th

Dear Mr Watson

I am writing this because I can't bring myself to speak to you. Why can't you control that stupid brute of a dog of yours? Or are you too thick to care what it does? Nearly every day it's in my garden, digging up the lawn and the flowerbeds and leaving its filthy messes everywhere. I've thrown stones and buckets of water at it whenever I've seen it but the brute takes no notice.

I give you fair warning that, if this goes on any longer, you'll be in trouble. Next time that dog comes into my garden, it's going to be sorry. My son has an air rifle. There are such things as rat poisons. One way or another I'm going to stop that dog from plaguing me, so you'd better keep it right out of my way.

And, if for some reason I can't stop it – I'll have the law on you. So you had better do something about it and quick.

John Smith

Letter B

4 Norton Drive
Weston

June 4th

Dear Mr Watson

I hope you don't mind me writing to you like this but I don't seem to see you about much these days.

The problem is that Bruce, your dog, has got into the habit of coming into our garden and digging. I know that you, being a gardener yourself, will sympathise when I tell you that, over the past week, we have lost two rose trees and about five dahlias, my wife's pride and joy, through Bruce's mining operations.

A better fence between us or putting Bruce on a free-run chain might be the answer but you may have better ideas. Could you ring me at 473 or call round some evening? I'd be grateful for a chat with you as soon as possible to sort things out.

Yours sincerely

John Smith

145

Step 13

In this Step you are shown how to:

■ write a funny story.

You are asked to:

■ consider what makes a story funny.

■ show your understanding of a passage called Setting Up Camp by answering questions of the kind you could be set in your exam.

■ discuss other pupils' written accounts of experiences of racialism and hooliganism.

■ write a letter and a report on the problems of camping and being in a strange place.

Writing

A funny story

Everyone has a funny story to tell — if he or she can remember it. These short extracts might remind you of a funny incident. Perhaps you can remember something that happened when you were younger, something that frightened you and now seems silly, looking back. Read this piece.

Counting the wrinkles

One time Petie came over to my house and told me he knew a way you could figure out when you were going to die — the very day! It was all according to the wrinkles in your hand. It took an hour to count them properly, and it came out I was going to die in my seventy-ninth year, on the eighty-third day.

Then we counted Petie's wrinkles. It came out he was going to die on the two hundred and seventy-ninth day of his ninth year. Well, Petie was nine years old right then, so he said, 'Get a calendar, quick, get a calendar,' and he looked like he was already getting sick.

We found an insurance calendar and started counting. I can still remember the terrible way it sounded when we both said 'Two hundred and seventy-nine.' Petie was going to die next Saturday.

I said, 'Let's do it again.' We did. It came out the same.

Petie had gone white.

'I better go home,' he said, like he meant, 'before something happens.'

from *The Midnight Fox* by Betsy Byars

The story develops over the next few days, until the crisis of Petie's 'death' day, and the party to celebrate his 'miraculous' survival.

The incident from your younger days need not be a near-disaster. In this piece a boy recalls filling his wellington boots with tadpoles.

Kes

You ought to have seen 'em, all black and shiny, right up to t'top. When we'd finished we kept dipping us fingers into 'em and whipping 'em up at each other, all shouting and excited like. Then this kid says to me, 'I bet tha daren't put one on.' And I says, 'I bet tha daren't.' So we said we'd put one on each. We wouldn't though, we kept reckoning to, then running away, so we tossed up and him who lost had to do it first. And I lost, oh, and you'd to take your socks off an' all. So I took my socks off, and I kept looking at this welli' full of taddies, and this kid kept saying, 'Go on then, tha frightened, tha frightened.' I was an' all. Anyway I shut my eyes and started to put my foot in. Oooo. It was just like putting your feet into live jelly. They were frozen. And when my foot went down, they all came over t'top of my wellington, and when I got my foot to t'bottom, I could feel 'em all squashing about between my toes.

Anyway I'd done it, and I says to this kid, 'Thee put thine on now.' But he wouldn't, he was dead scared, so I put it on instead. I'd got used to it then, it was all right after a bit; it sent your legs all excited and tingling like. When I'd got 'em both on I started to walk up to this kid, waving my arms and making spook noises; and as I walked they all came squelching over t'tops again and ran down t'sides. This kid looked frightened to death, he kept looking down at my wellies so I tried to run at him and they all spurted up my legs. You ought to have seen him. He just screamed out and ran home roaring.

It was a funny feeling though when he'd gone; all quiet, with nobody there, and up to t'knees in tadpoles.

from *Kes* by Barry Hines

Notice how the dialogue, particularly the Yorkshire accent, is important for the effect of the piece.

This following piece shows one good source of humour – how we tend to laugh at other people's troubles but don't find our own troubles funny. Three young men are on a boating holiday.

Three men in a boat

While I was dressing that morning, I had my back to the boat. It was nearly freezing and in the hurry to get my shirt on I accidentally dropped it in the river. I started swearing and George started laughing. I couldn't see anything to laugh at, and I told him to shut up, but he only laughed more. He had to sit down in the end. He'd become weak at the knees laughing at me. Turning blue and trying to fish the shirt out with a stick I pointed out what a drivelling maniac and imbecile idiot he was; he just laughed louder. And then, just as I was landing the shirt, I noticed it wasn't one of mine at all. It was his: I'd been trying to put it on by mistake. The funny side of it now struck me for the first time, and I began to laugh. I laughed so much I let the shirt slip back into the water.

'Aren't you going to get it out?' said George, between sniggers.

'I don't think so. It's not my shirt; it's yours.' I never saw a man's face change so quickly.

'What!' he yelled, springing up. 'You clumsy idiot. Why can't you be more careful? You're not fit to be on a boat. Get that shirt out.'

I tried to make him see the funny side of it, but he just raged at me. Sometimes George is very dense at seeing a joke.

from *Three Men in a Boat* by Jerome K. Jerome

'Do-it-yourself' has always been a source of humour. Read this piece by someone your own age.

A cheap repair!

It cost about eighty pounds to replace the pane of glass that my dad broke by slamming it. It would have been cheaper to have a gang of workmen, but my dad decided he'd save money by doing it himself in what he said would be 'next to no time'.

First time he measured the pane wrong; it just fell through and smashed. Next day he tried again. He dropped it. Of course, he blamed me for not opening the car door wide enough. The pane we eventually got fixed in had bloodstains on it; he 'found' a piece of the old glass he hadn't taken out.

Colin (15)

The piece hasn't worked because the writer hasn't included enough detail. Opportunities for dialogue have been missed and the reader would like to know more about the author's father and his reaction.

Write your own funny story

■ Keep the story to about 300 words. A true account will work best. Record the event in detail and include some conversation. What could you write about the picture below?

SELF ASSESSMENT

Ask your teacher to read out all the pieces without giving the names of the authors. Mark out of ten for funniness.

Understanding

Read the following piece about an adventure. The writer and her friend and assistant, Annie, made a wild-life film for television on one of the smaller Falkland Islands. This passage is taken from her book about her experiences.

■ Then answer the questions that follow. They are the type of questions you will be asked in your exam.

Setting up camp

It took us several days to sort out camp. Having removed all the things we found in the hut and stored them safely in a shed, we set about scrubbing it out before unpacking our equipment. It was quite a nice little hut – ten foot square – with two beds, a table, two chairs, a gas fire,
5 running water heated by gas and a chemical loo. There was one large window facing north, which, in the southern hemisphere, is the sunny side and this made the hut terribly hot on sunny days but, without insulation, it was bitterly cold on wet days, with the little gas fire making no difference. The heat went straight out through the thin roof. The window
10 still wouldn't open, no matter how hard we tried, which meant that, at night, we had to leave the door open to get some air. More than once we woke up to find a two-foot snow drift in the middle of the room. However, it was dry and well built and was going to be our home for the next six months . . .
15 During that first week, the sun shone every day but the winds blew, sometimes up to sixty miles an hour. The black-browed albatross had already arrived at the colony at the top of the hill behind the hut. They were busy building up their tall mud nests and going through their courtship display and mating. Down at the south end of the island, the
20 gentoo penguins had also arrived and were busy building their simple nests of stone and grass, mating and calling to each other all the time. We put up a small tent near their colony so that if it suddenly turned nasty with rain or snow when we were filming them, we would have somewhere to take shelter.
25 Annie had never put up a tent before and though willing to try anything once, almost managed to strangle herself in all the guy ropes as the tent tried to take off in the strong wind. That first week was sheer hell. We had to carry all our heavy camera equipment up and down the hills battling against the wind. Our legs and backs hated every moment of it all
30 until they finally got used to it. But it was the wind that really tired us out. Walking into the sixty mph wind, carrying thirty pounds on our backs, was no fun. The force of the wind literally drove the breath out of us, leaving us gasping like fish out of water. It could stop us in our tracks and even, on occasion, force us back again. Climbing over the rocks was slow

35 and difficult work as we were easily caught off balance. The bitter cold left
our hands, feet and faces numb and after several hours of sitting with the
birds we would develop violent shivering attacks. By the end of each day
we were utterly exhausted.

Annie found it all very difficult to start with. The first fence she had to
40 climb over she split her trousers. She cut herself so often with her new
penknife that we ran out of sticking plaster in the first week and I had to
take the penknife away from her.

During those first few weeks on New Island, she seemed to fall over
every rock and clump of grass she could find but as the weeks went by
45 she gradually got the hang of it and became much more nimble on her
feet. Every Sunday, we would take the morning off to wash our hair and
clothes. The first time we hung out the clothes to dry we found most of
them missing after half an hour. The wind had blown them away and we
had to go over the island collecting socks and bras that had been blown
50 into gorse bushes and ditches or had been caught on old barbed-wire
fences.

from *Survival: South Atlantic by Cindy Buxton and Annie Price*

1 How can you tell that, when the two women arrived, they thought the shed was rather dirty? (1)

2 If you didn't already know, what two words in the first paragraph would tell you that the Falkland Islands are well below the equator? (2)

3 What do you understand by the word 'insulation' in the first paragraph? (2)

4 Explain briefly the ventilation problem they had in the hut. What further problem did they sometimes have when they had solved this first one? (3)

5 As briefly as you can, name the two kinds of bird mentioned in the second paragraph and describe the preparations each made for rearing their young. (4)

6 Mention three things that suggest that Annie was rather clumsy when she first came to the island. (3)

7 What three things made the moving of equipment 'sheer hell'? (3)

8 What single word in the last paragraph shows that Annie was much more skilful about clambering over rocks and grass as time went by? (1)

9 What evidence is there in the next to the last and the last paragraph that there had been some farming on the island? (2)

10 Which of these two phrases seem to best describe the writer's attitude in the passage: 'very serious' or 'reasonably light-hearted'. Give some evidence from the passage to support your answer. (4)

Oral work

Read these two pieces.

A

The experience which changed my view about racialism happened after the football match between Juventus and Liverpool. I was in France on an exchange at the time. Like most other teenagers I was very anti-Pakastani, if your friends didn't like 'Pakkies' – as we called them – then
5 you didn't either I never thought of myself as racialist but now I relise I was. I've never had any hatred towards blacks or Italians, Jews or any other race, just Pakistanis.

It was the day after the horrific scenes in Brussels when the Liverpool football fans rioted and many Italians were killed. I was feeling extremely
10 ashamed to be British – like many other members of our school party. We had a trip arranged to a small port called Le Croisic, the day began perfectly, the weather was hot and everyone was in high spirits despite the antics of the previous night. We reached Le Croisic and went our seperate ways, Angela came with me and we decided to go shopping for
15 souvenirs. We walked into a small gift shop and were brousing around, just looking for presents, the shop-owner approached Angela and I and asked in broken English 'Are you British?' We both nodded. 'Then get out of my shop. We were hearded or escorted to the door, call it what you want. We stared at each other in disbelief, neither of us could
20 understand the reasoning behind this man's behaviour, then I realised it must be because of the football, I was so incensed what right did he have for being so rude? I don't even watch football on television, never mind go along to matches. We received the same reception in two more shops and then decided to give up and return to the rendezvous at the station.
25 Others in the party had been given the same reception, one girl had been spat at. I was livid and stood and complained, then the teacher said 'That's racialism'. I stopped and thought about this statement, so this was how the Pakistanis felt, what had they done to me? Nothing yet still I hated them and antagonised them at every chance. The group returned to
30 England, but that one incident has made me think twice about annoying the Pakistanis, to begin with I stopped myself from being racialist but you soon forget and now once again like all my friends, I'm back into my anti-Paki state of mind, but I still stop now and again and think of the French shop-owner in the little fishing port of Le Croisic.

J (16)

B

It was the day of the F.A. cup quater final Luton were to be playing
Millwall. I had been warned before I set off to Luton with my friend that I
should be careful. But I just explained that its not dangerous and there's
no such thing as football hooligans they are just made up by people who
5   don't like football. I hadn't been worried at all before the match it never
crossed my mind that there might be some trouble. The way I had always
looked at the problem of hooliganism was that you won't get hurt if you
stand well back and don't shout to much that way you don't irritate
anyone. I personally always sort of worshipped these big lads, who didn't
10   seem to have a worry about anything, standing on the terraces shouting
with such exuberance.

I qued up waiting to get in still there was no trouble not even a sign of
violence. Inside the ground I could hear the Luton supporters chanting
'Wem . . . ber . . ly, Wem-ber-ly – we're the famous Lu – on Town and
15   we're going to Wembly.'

The crowd were in great spirites. After being frisked I went into the
stand it was crowded I could hardly see the pitch at all. We decided to try
and get a bit closer to the pitch.

In the away end some of the Millwall supporters appeared to be
20   climbing over the fence. It started with just a few but then hundreds of
these men came sprinting scross the pitch chanting and swearing. The
Luton supporters went quite, never before had I been so scared. The
men, well they were only about sixteen were wearing really respectable
clothes. They looked so neat and tidy you would never suspect them of
25   hooliganism. They were just wearing just ordinary bleached jeans a pair of
expensive trainers, and a jumper or a tracksuit top.

As they got nearer the Luton crowd began to back up. I can
remember one old man shouting at two stewards and policewoman to
arrest three hundred rioting hooligans.
30   The Millwall supporters then turned to the seated area, they ran into
this area still shouting and swearing and then with great joy and pleasure
proceeded in ripping the seats out and hurling them at the Luton
supporters. Now fully armed they charged once more towards us this time
skimming coins, hurling bits of plastic seat and even throwing pool balls.
35   This was about enough for me I felt sick to see lads of only a year, or
less, older than me rioting I was petrified. The game hadn't even started
yet. My point of view had changed completely when I arrived I expected
there to be a nice friendly atmosphere, and had told my mum that
hooligans are something that you read about in comics but now it had
40   happened to me I had seen it myself and it made me shake with fear. We
were so disgusted that we went home before the match finished. Luton
one in the end but it wasn't much consilation.

T (16)

Discuss racial bias and hooliganism

These two pieces were written by people of your age in answer to the question: 'Write about an event which changed your point of view.'

■ Use them as a basis for discussing racial bias and hooliganism. Consider these points:

From A
The writer admits to racial bias herself, but at the end of the piece she says she often *thinks* about her experience in France.
Is racial bias a result of people not stopping to think?
Had the French any reason to abuse the English schoolchildren?
Why did they abuse them? Was it fear, dislike, a need to blame somebody?
What does the writer mean by 'I don't even watch football on television, let alone go to matches'?
How does this feeling apply to all victims of racialism?

From B
Unlike so many people who talk about football hooliganism, the writer has obviously had personal experience.
What shows that he was actually there rather than making up a story?
What surprised the writer about the appearance of the rioters? What surprised him about their age and behaviour?
What can you learn from this piece about the causes of the problem?
What are your solutions?

Note
Both pieces have been reproduced exactly as they were written.
Pick out the errors in both pieces.
Do the spelling and other mistakes affect your response to the writing? Did you notice them as you read through the pieces? If you did then your response to the meaning is bound to be slightly altered – for a moment you stop thinking about what is being said.

Remember this in your own writing.

Spotlight on skills

☆ ☆ ☆ ☆ ☆ ☆ ☆ ☆ ☆ ☆
Spelling – some advice

1 Learn to spell the words you have spelled incorrectly. Learn ten a day from a few weeks before the examination so they are fresh in your mind.
2 Make a particular list of your common errors – the words you spell wrongly most times.
3 Make sure you can spell these words:

a lot (two words)   does   goes   clothes (not cloths)   until   coming   tried frightened   heard   really   disappear stopped   surprise   happened   among believe   disgusting   first   having   idea

4 Make a list of words you confuse: for example, now and know, quite and quiet.
5 Always use the best word whether you can spell it or not. Don't just use the easy words.
6 Here are some useful rules:

knock off the **e** for **ing**: **hope, hoping**.
words end **ly** and not **ley**: **immediately**.
ful words end with one **l**: **beautiful**.
i before **e** except after **c** if the sound is **EE**: eg, **believe, receive**; for all other sounds, eg, **AY** 'ei' as in weight.

believe
receipt
disappear
clothes

■ From your list of errors see how many you can put in one sentence: I had a big **surprise** when I found out how many of my **clothes** had **disappeared**.

157

Communication

Directed writing – letter and report

■ Read **Setting up camp** on pages 151 and 152 again and then . . .

1 How much do you think Annie liked her first days on the island? Write a letter to a friend as if you were Annie, describing your experiences and how you felt.

2 Have you ever had the experience of moving house, of caravanning or camping, or staying in a holiday home? Write an account of one of these or of any other experience you have had of your first days in a new place.

3 You, too, are about to stay on an almost uninhabited island with none of the usual amenities of modern life such as doctors, shops or roads. Write a report of how you would prepare for such an experience.

Each piece should be about 200 words.

Step 14

In this Step you are shown how to:

■ write about a childhood experience.

You are asked to:

■ do a multiple choice passage for understanding.
■ take a role in arranging a visit by telephone.
■ revise the skills studied in the book and fill in a skills' profile.
■ write reports and letters about a council meeting.

Writing

Professional authors write a great deal about their childhood. Although you are still young there are things that have happened to you that other people would like to read about, particularly early fears. Here a girl of twelve has a frightening experience:

A frightening experience

When you are twelve years old and you look seventeen you're bound to get into trouble! This happened several years ago, yet I can still remember every detail, every feeling, as though it were yesterday.

5   My parents had reluctantly allowed me to work in a hospital during the summer vacation. Because I not only looked responsible but was responsible for my years, I was asked to replace Agathe Hogue as cleaning woman in the 'Post Mortem' room. The words 'post mortem' are enough to frighten any fully matured individual; imagine the impact of a visit to such a place when you are a sensitive pre-teenager!

10   The first morning of cleaning was shocking but the presence of Agathe who was initiating me, was reassuring. Both of us washed the table on which the operation had just been performed. If the old grave diggers' tales about burying some people alive are true, then I can safely say that the autopsy ascertains death and prevents the so-called dead from 'living'

15   through a horrible 'grave' experience! The table we washed was a framed screen wire placed over a tub. The screen allowed the passage of blood and small parts of the body cut during the autopsy. I was cold and sick and frightened but I was proud, too. They had chosen me and I couldn't let them see how young and inadequate I really was! We also washed

20   tools but did not sterilise them. Germs cannot affect the dead!

Agathe left at noon for her holidays. During my lunch hour, at home, I played with my dolls; they were so safe. At one o'clock I was back in the hospital where I was asked to go to the 'room', the 'P.M.' room, as it was called, and place clean glass tubes in a jug of solution. The door didn't

25   squeak as I opened it but the cold air of the room slapped me across the face. I just couldn't go in. I walked in the hall for a minute or two, then reasoned myself into going back.

Inside, I saw twelve small closed refrigerator doors. One of them contained a body, the body of Mrs F. Johnson. Her name was written on

30   a small blackboard by the door . . . Tools, jugs, tubes, machinery, all lined the wall facing the door. With a cold trembling hand and heart and body, I tried to place a tray of tubes in a glass jug. The tubes fell on the floor, shattered to pieces. Like a frightened fawn I ran out of the room, out of the ward, out of the hospital, into a park and there, on a bench, I

35   sat facing the hospital with wide glassy eyes for six long empty hours . . .

from Very Nice, Very Nice, by Annette Tencha

■ Discuss the writing in small groups.

1 What makes the writing seem real?
2 Why is it possibly more frightening than if the writer had made up a ghost story?
3 Should the girl have been allowed to work there?
4 Should children be protected from the grim realities of life?

Write about your own childhood

■ Put as much feeling and detail to make it seem true into one of these titles. You should write about 400 words:

1 The most frightening day of my life *or* some frightening things that have happened to me
2 Growing up in a strange place (or country)
3 When I most upset my mother (or father)
4 The fun that went wrong
5 Things I still feel guilty about
6 Events and people that have had the greatest influence on me
7 Primary school (or the new school)
8 The day I was lost

SELF ASSESSMENT

Compare your writing with the earliest piece you can find that you did on this course. Pencil in a mark out of 20 for improvement.

Some final advice on writing

In this book we have shown you the various kinds of writing we think you can do best. We have tried to steer you away from sensational crime and science fiction because most people of your age cannot write them well. If you do have a talent for them, your teacher will tell you. It is also unwise to write about what you have seen on film or television as this will lead to second-hand writing lacking in feeling, sensitivity and freshness, the qualities your examiners are looking for.

Understanding

Multiple choice

Read the following passage carefully. Do not let the hard words put you off.

A fateful time

When I said that 1960 was a fateful time I did not mean only that it was decisive for my future as a writer; an event occured in that year that still haunts me and will continue to haunt me for the rest of my days. Jo, you may remember, was pregnant on our return from the short holiday in
5   Paris, and, as she grew monstrously big, her doctor began to wonder how many babies she was carrying. Manipulation suggested that there were twins and an X-ray confirmed their presence.

    After the initial mild hysteria that the knowledge caused, we quickly grew accustomed to the prospect of having two more children instead of
10   one, and we started to prepare ourselves by acquiring, second-hand, a twin pram and an extra cot and deciding on two girls' names and two boys' so that we would be armed whatever sex or mixture of sexes the twins turned out to be.

    The winter gave way to spring and Jo grew closer to the time of her
15   confinement which was to take place in Redhill Hospital. On the day that the ambulance carried her away I took Jane and Nancy over to their grandparents at Edenbridge where we were all staying for a few days and, early next morning, I telephoned the hospital.

    I held the receiver to my ear and heard the mechanical jets of noise in
20   the darkness, the quick double rasps, repeated four or five times. Then a voice said, 'Redhill Hospital. Can I help you?'

    I asked for the maternity ward.

    A few moments later another woman's voice came on the line. I told her who I was and asked for news of Jo and the twins. She seemed to
25   hesitate for a fraction of a second before she answered and I felt, even then, a cold tremor of uncertainty, a blind premonition of misfortune.

    She said, 'Mrs Scannell has given birth to twin boys.' Again that slight hesitation. 'The first baby is perfectly healthy, but I'm afraid that the other . . . is not quite . . .' She hurried on: 'we think the best thing would be
30   for you to come and see the doctor. He'll explain everything.'

    I said, 'You mean he's deformed?'

    'I'm sorry, Mr Scannell, I can't really give any details. I simply don't know anything except that one baby is not as well as he should be. You come to the hospital and speak to the doctor. He'll tell you everything.'
35   'When can I come?'

    'Could you be here at ten o'clock this morning?'

I said that I could and rang off. I felt dazed and sickened, very much as if I had taken a heavy punch under the heart. Jo's mother was hovering anxiously and I realised she must have heard me use the word
40 'deformed'. I told her the little I knew and she, too, looked stunned and wretched and I thought – though this may only have been my own feeling of irrational guilt – a little accusing.

I tried to reassure her. 'It might not be too bad. The woman didn't seem to know much·about it.'

45 She nodded, but she was not listening, and I thought, not for the first time, that women always take the heaviest punishment. She set about preparing breakfast for Jane and Nancy and I went to my room and smoked until my mouth was parched and bitter. I tried not to keep looking at my watch. I went out into the garden where the apple trees
50 were in blossom and the birds were jubilant in the morning sun. I tried not to think about the deformed baby but I could not prevent the images from invading the mind, images spawned by scraps of gossip, half-remembered and probably untrue in the first place, of human monsters, alive but hidden from public view in special hospitals and asylums,
55 obscenities with the heads of rodents on scaly bodies, huge cyclopic heads on tiny trunks, malformations of hands and feet, a faceless head, a living bladder of lard with orifices only for breathing and eating. When I tried to tell myself that I was almost certainly exaggerating the affliction of my baby, that he was most likely only suffering from some minor
60 disfiguration or handicap, I found that my mind swung away from more comfortable speculation to welcome back the nightmare images, because it dared not face the possibility that the reality might be worse than the imagined condition.

At half-past nine I borrowed my father-in-law's car and drove to the
65 hospital. I was a little early but the doctor saw me straight away. He was a dark, tired-looking man, mercifully unfussy and practical.

He said, 'I'm afraid this is an unpleasant shock for you. As you know, one of the babies seems to be perfectly normal. A normal delivery, quite an easy one. The second wasn't so easy. He's suffering from what is
70 called meningocele, that's a hernia of the meninges, the membranes over the brain and spinal cord. He's got a big swelling on the back of his head and this will have to be removed. I think the chances of his surviving are pretty good but how much brain damage he's likely to suffer I couldn't say. I'm not a specialist on this, you see. But I know enough about it to
75 say that the damage might be very considerable indeed. Encephalitis is common with these cases and you can be certain that the child will never be able to lead a normal life. I'd go as far as to say that it's very doubtful that he'll be able to walk or talk, though – as I've said – you must wait for a specialist opinion before you decide what you're going to do.'

from *Tiger and the Rose* by Vernon Scannell

What you have to do

■ Write the number of each question and then write beside it the letter of the answer you think is correct. Only one answer can be right for each question.

1 The event that haunted the writer was:
   a the birth of twins
   b the wife becoming pregnant
   c the birth of a deformed baby
   d his wife growing monstrously big   (1)

2 Twins were confirmed by:
   a manipulation
   b an X-ray
   c mild hysteria
   d his wife growing big   (1)

3 One of these was **not** done to prepare for the birth of twins:
   a a twin pram was bought
   b an extra cot was bought
   c both girls' and boys' names were decided on
   d the parents looked up some knowledge to help them   (1)

4 You first realise something is wrong when:
   a the telephone rasps four or five times
   b a voice said, 'Redhill Hospital. Can I help you?'
   c the woman's voice hesitates for a fraction of a second
   d the man asks for news of the twins   (1)

5 The news of the babies is:
   a they both have something wrong with them
   b one is healthy, one is not
   c they are a boy and a girl
   d they are identical twins   (1)

6 The author may have once been a boxer because:
   a he felt dazed
   b he was used to heavy punishment   (1)
   c he felt as if he had taken a blow under the heart
   d he was stunned

7 The author tries to calm himself by:
   a saying the baby is deformed to Jo's mother
   b saying it might not be too bad
   c not looking at his watch
   d smoking heavily   (1)

8 He goes into the garden:
   a to listen to the birds sing
   b to try to calm himself
   c to look at the apple blossom
   d to think about monsters   (1)

9 One of these images does **not** come into his mind:
   a the head of a rodent
   b a huge head and a tiny body
   c a faceless head
   d an elephant's head   (1)

10 He tries to tell himself that he is exaggerating by:
   a thinking it was only a minor handicap
   b thinking of his baby breathing and eating
   c thinking that something may only be wrong with its bladder
   d listening to the birds   (1)

11 The doctor sees him right away because:
   a he had come in a car
   b he arrived at 9.30 am
   c he wants to tell him the truth quickly
   d his father-in-law was with him   (1)

12 The doctor's first remark was:
   a I'm afraid this is an unpleasant shock for you
   b one of the babies seems to be perfectly normal
   c he's suffering from meningocele
   d he's got a big swelling on the back of his head   (1)

13 The operation he mentions is about:
   a operating on the spinal cord
   b removing the swelling in the back of the head
   c repairing the brain damage
   d giving him a new meningocele   (1)

14 The baby is likely to:
   a survive
   b be able to walk
   c be able to talk
   d lead a normal life   (1)

15 The author must:
   a consult two other doctors
   b consult a specialist
   c make up his mind immediately
   d ask his wife   (1)

16 Which words best describe the tone of this passage:
   a a sense of outrage
   b uncertainty of feeling
   c a wild hysteria
   d constant worry   (1)

17 The author is a man because:
   a he knows nothing about the birth of babies
   b he talks about his wife
   c he writes about boxing
   d he writes in a male way   (1)

18 Most people would want to read the next part of this:
   a to find out more about the mother
   b to find out what happened to the baby
   c to find out about the other twin
   d to learn more about childbirth   (1)

19 Which of these is the best clue that the author is not wealthy:
   a he has only had a short holiday in Paris
   b he borrows his father-in-law's car
   c he has two children already
   d he buys a second-hand pram   (1)

20 We know the author had a vivid imagination because of:
   a the things he imagines in the garden
   b the fact that he gets hysterical about twins
   c the way he describes the doctor
   d the fact that he thinks of both boys' and girls' names   (1)

Oral work

The telephone

Read these instructions carefully.

The secretary to the Managing Director of Worldspan, a London firm that makes communications equipment, has been left with this task.

A party of Japanese, three men and two women, is visiting your company for two days. They will arrive at Heathrow Airport at 5 p.m. on Wednesday, 6th June, and their return flight is at 10 a.m. on Saturday, 9th June. The manager wants you to arrange for them to be met at the airport, taken to a hotel and fetched to Worldspan's offices at 10 a.m. on 7th June, where they will spend the morning with him.
The Japanese also wish to look round the factory, see a play in the West End and have a guided tour of the Tower of London. They will eat at the hotel, except lunch on Wednesday and Thursday when they will have lunch at Worldspan offices.

■ Four people should take turns to be the secretary, making the necessary calls to plan the visit. Taking notes and previous planning is essential.

There are ten other parts (including Managing Director), that can be shared round the rest of the class, changing for each new secretary.

Acourts Taxis
Bolam Taxi Service
Grand Hotel
Royal Court Playhouse
Roxy Theatre
Chandlers Theatre
Tower of London Information Desk

The secretary may contact these people on the internal telephone:

Peter Stewart – Works Manager (He shows people round the factory)
Emma Gordon – in charge of the catering

The people taking these ten parts will also need to prepare. The secretary at the taxi services will need to know whether taxis are available at the times needed. The hotels will need to know availability and prices of their rooms. The theatres will need to know what is being performed, times, prices – they may be asked how suitable the play is for foreign visitors.

Notes
1 Mime holding the telephone and do not look at the person you are ringing.
2 Do not make things too easy for the secretary, but do not be too difficult. Each hotel should, for instance, have some rooms free on the correct nights, but it's not unreasonable for there not to be quite enough. The secretary may even have to send the visitors to different hotels, or even have to make two of them share a double room.

Each secretary should make an outline, with dates and times, of the plan for the visit when she or he has finished telephoning.

Spotlight on skills

☆ ☆ ☆ ☆ ☆ ☆ ☆ ☆ ☆ ☆ ☆

Revision work

1 Look in a dictionary to find out the meaning of these prefixes:

ultra   pre   psycho   hydro   mis

2 Each of these words has been used in this book. But you may need to look them up in a dictionary. Put each in a sentence of your own:

literally   dilapidated   gesticulate
nostalgia   fluctuation   contrasting
pathetic   contaminated   accomplished
pitfalls

3 Punctuate this into sentences, put in any capitals and divide into two paragraphs:

the summer had been the worst aziz could remember rain seemed to have fallen continously since april his mother and father had taken over this small guest house at st annes they needed to be booked up each week to make much of a profit but people had begun to cancel their holidays and other people were not taking up the cancellations to make matters worse his brother had fallen out with him it began as a petty quarrel over a present for their mother aziz wanted to give her flowers but his brother wanted to spend a big sum on a brooch that aziz could not afford

4 Put this into speech punctuation. Put in capitals, question marks, any exclamation marks, apostrophes commas and full-stops:

give it some choke said atifa its an automatic one said sanjay well why wont it start its been a cold night but it should start oh no what is it theres no petrol in exclaimed sanjay i bet it was tim taking home those girls last night he tried once more but the engine was dead

5 There are many words ending with **s** in this piece but only a few of them need the apostrophe for ownership. Which are they? Punctuate also into sentences and put in capitals and commas:

there was no doubt that mr lings shop was doing well for a start he was open seven days a week he seemed to stock everything you could get a dogs collar tea bags plasters for corns or single fuses on thursdays he always held a sale when he sold off things he was not shifting pennys uncle mick once found some glasses for 10p when his were broken by angies baby

6 Write these sentences to check your skills:

a one with a name of a cinema and a film in it

b one about the weather with two apostrophes for omission

c one in which a dog belongs to Mr Smith and a cat belongs to Miss Jones (use apostrophes for ownership)

d one in which you use a new word you have learned this month

e one in which a doctor visits a patient in an old street in a town near you (see capitals for names and places)

f one in which a friend asks you a question and you answer it (use speech punctuation)

g write a list of five things to take on a holiday in a single sentence

h one in which you name a car, a bike and a river

i write down as a sentence what this word means: contiguous

j write down in speech punctuation the conversation of three people watching a film they do not like

Give yourself a mark out of 10 for how good you are at each of these skills. Do not mark this book.

Skills profile

Sentence punctuation	Writing a personal letter
Capital letters	Writing a business letter
Comma for a slight pause	Writing my opinions
Commas for lists	Writing a story
Speech punctuation	Writing about my experiences
The question mark	Writing a description
Apostrophe for omission	Writing about my feelings
Apostrophe for ownership	Writing a report
Paragraphing	Writing a summary
Using a dictionary	Giving a talk
Leaning new words	Discussing in a group
Understanding a piece of writing	Reading aloud (including plays)

Communication

A council meeting

Scene: The council chamber of the Worlington District Council. All the councillors have assembled for a very important debate. The ruling party on the council propose to privatise the bus service which is at present run by the council on a subsidy. There are many interested spectators in the public gallery. The Chairperson for the meeting rises.

Chairperson   We all know why we are here. I won't bore you all by giving you a history of the bus service in this borough. I'll come straight to the point. We believe we will get a more efficient and cheaper bus service if it ceases to be run by the council and is put out to private tender. We think we can save £400,000 in a full year and cut the local rate by 2p.

Councillor Soggs   When do you propose to do this?

Chairperson   If the vote goes that way this afternoon, we will advertise for tender on the first of September. This will give us time to wind up the council controlled service.

Councillor Ali   You mean sack bus drivers who have given loyal service to this district for years.

Chairperson   We think they will be absorbed into the private services.

Councillor Ali   You must be joking. We know that other authorities that have done this have caused seventy-five per cent of their busdrivers to go on the dole to add to the millions already there.

Chairperson   I was not aware of that. If your figure is correct it shows how those services must have been over-manned, costing the ratepayers a great deal of money.

Councillor Ali   Are you disputing my figures?

Chairperson   I would question their source.

Councillor Ali   My figures are all too accurate.

Councillor Neckton   Don't let's get into a fruitless argument about figures. Let's think of the service to the public. Any reader of the *Worlington Gazette* will know the number of complaints about the buses: buses not on time; rude drivers; cancelled services. I'm sure a private service will be more efficient.

Councillor Barnes   It'll be efficient all right, in the rush hour. I've come from a district that's done this. The place is knee-deep in buses during the rush hour but at off-peak times you couldn't find a bus for love or money.

Councillor Davies	I represent a rural area as you well know. My constituents are worried that they will get no buses at all except on Saturdays.
Chairperson	We have a plan to work with the post office as they do in Scotland and a few other areas to use mini buses. We see no point in providing, as at present, fifty-seater buses for a few people.
Councillor Barnes	Can the Chair assure me that bus passes for old age pensioners will still be issued for the private buses?
Chairperson	That is under review.
Councillor Soggs	You know that's to be one of the cuts.
Chairperson	I don't know. As I say it's under review.
Councillor Soggs	Pull the other leg.
Councillor Neckton	Please Councillor Soggs, if the Chair says it is under review it means just that.
Councillor Simons	I must support the Chair. I have been on some excellent coach tours with local private companies. I'm sure they could provide excellent local services.
Councillor Ali	Yes, but how much will the fares go up?
Councillor Simons	The coach tours were very cheap.
Voices from gallery	We protest! We protest! Keep our buses! Keep our buses!
Another voice	Doesn't your brother own a local coach firm, Councillor Simons?
Chairperson	Please! Please!
Voices	Keep our buses. Keep our buses.
	(There is an uproar in the gallery with banner waving. The Chairperson calls for the police. The gallery is cleared and after ten minutes the debate is resumed. In the voting at the end of the debate the Council votes by 35 votes to 20 to go ahead and privatise the bus service.)

What you have to do

■ Using reported speech write a report of the meeting from the moment Councillor Neckton begins to speak. Use expressions like Councillor Neckton **said that**, **stated that**, **believed that**. This play is in the present tense. Make sure your report is in the past tense. Your report should go to the point where the gallery is cleared.

Write a letter – your point of view

■ Using your home address write a letter to the Worlington Gazette giving your point of view on the matter. You can use arguments you have read in the play. Set out your letter properly.

■ Making up an address and signing your letter 'Angry Rate-payer' write a letter to the same newspaper which has exactly the opposite views to yours.

Each letter should contain no more than 150 words of content, excluding the address etc.

A newspaper report favouring privatisation

The following report of the meeting appeared in the *Worlington Gazette*:

Outrageous scenes in council chamber
Police called to evict rowdies. Man arrested

Appalling scenes took place in the Worlington District Council chamber last Thursday at the end of a debate on the local bus services. Bearded left-wing trendies waved banners and shouted obscenities in an attempt to prevent a full debate on this important issue.

The council has been worried for some time now at the drain on the ratepayers' pockets of the heavily subsidised local bus service. The Chairperson opened by rightly explaining that there could be a saving of £400,000 and a better bus service could result.

Councillor Ali expressed concern over redundancies but the Chairperson explained that bus drivers would be absorbed into the new private services and that a slimming down operation was needed anyway in an over-manned service. Councillor Ali got very heated over this but the Chairperson remained cool throughout the debate.

Councillor Neckton mentioned the number of complaints this newspaper had received about the present services. Indeed there is one today on Page 6.

Councillor Barnes has come from an area where a private bus service is already working efficiently. He explained that there was always a good service in the rush hour.

Councillor Mrs Elsie Davies expressed the only real concern which was the fate of the rural service, an issue this newspaper has campaigned upon for years. The Chairperson said that an arrangement was being discussed with the Post Office about the use of their mini-buses, something that has always been opposed by officials of the subsidised service.

At that point in the debate when Councillor Soggs brought up the irrelevant issue of cuts there was a disturbance in the public gallery. Councillor Simons was shouted down. The Chairperson, however, remained cool and had the gallery cleared.

A man was arrested outside for jostling the Chairperson as he left.

The council voted by 35 votes to 20 to adopt the policy of privatisation.

What you have to do

Both papers use bias (one-sided) and emotive words (words to arouse your feeling) to support the side of the argument they take.

■ Pick out four emotive words or sentences from the report in the *Gazette* and four from the *Banner*. Say which side each paper supports.

■ Pick out three incidents from each report where the truth has been bent to suit the paper's views

■ One issue raised by a person in the public gallery has not been mentioned at all by either paper. Why might this be? If one paper dared to mention it which one would it be?

■ Now write a report of the meeting in not more than 200 words which is completely fair and does not take sides.

172

A newspaper report opposing privatisation

The following report appeared in the *Worlington Banner*, a newspaper run by people on a local council estate:

MANY JOBS THREATENED
Public protest at council decision
Cowardly bus pass threat

The shadow of government thinking over local issues loomed over the Worlington District Council's meeting to decide the fate of local bus services.

The mockery of a debate was interrupted by peaceful protesters who demanded that a full council-backed local bus service was kept for the benefit of all the citizens of the Worlington area.

The feeling was so strong that the protest continued outside the meeting chamber. A man was arrested for accidentally bumping into a policeman who was walking in front of the Chairperson.

The debate started by the Chairperson putting the mythical view that vast savings could be made at no cost to local services by privatising the buses and saving a measly few pence on the rates.

Councillor Ali valiantly defended the jobs of local bus drivers. He stated that in other areas where this folly had been tried 75% of busmen had been sacked, adding to the millions already on the dole.

Councillor Neckton brought up the red-herring of letters to the Gazette about bus services. This was quickly dealt with by Councillor Barnes who stated that a private bus service would only run at peak times inconveniencing people who wanted to travel at other hours.

Councillor Mrs Elsie Davies expressed the tremendous concern in the rural areas that they would have no bus service at all for six days of the week. The Chairperson's reply to this was that people could ride in mail vans with the parcels and letters. A fine way for people to travel who have few enough amenities as it is.

An issue that the Chairperson had kept concealed was brought to light by Councillor Barnes. As well as a threat to the services there was also a threat to the bus passes for old age pensioners.

Councillor Soggs felt that this was one of the government cuts threatening council's services.

The thought of old people confined to their homes by a mean council was just too much for some people in the public gallery who protested peacefully. They were roughly ejected from the chamber by the police on the orders of the Chairperson.

Afterwards the council voted by 35 votes to 20 to privatise the bus service, the so-called independents joining with the ruling party in this farce of a debate.

Your coursework folio C

An examination paper asks you to complete a piece of writing in a set time. You do not know the subject before you open the paper. Some writing for your folio will have to be done in a set time under examination conditions, but you will probably have been given time to prepare your material beforehand. Other pieces for your folio will be of your own choice. You will have much longer to prepare and you will write them in your own time.

Coursework gives you more time. It tests not only your ability but the effort you are prepared to make. You should be prepared to do some research on your subject in the library. You should also take pains to re-draft your material until you are satisfied you have made the best effort you can. Be prepared to think out and plan your piece before you start.

These notes will help you to make sure your folio is as good as you can make it.

Writing a story

Your own experiences
Most people write best about their own experiences, and everybody has at least one interesting tale to tell. Tell the reader about the people in your story. A story is always more interesting if you know the people involved.

Types of story
You may like to write a story of a particular type, a ghost or science-fiction story, for instance. Try to make your story original and avoid cliché (over-used expressions or ideas).

Factual writing
Variety in your folder is important. A clearly written and well-organised piece of factual writing will provide a good contrast to creative writing. A set of instructions for carrying out a process you are interested in (taking and developing film, for instance) would be ideal, but you must make sure the instructions are based on your own experiences.

Evaluative writing
You should include at least one piece making a judgement, drawing your own conclusions. This may be in the form of a report about a holiday, an assessment of a particular

computer, or even something more complex such as the changes you would make in your school. Your report could be the result of a survey you have done in your class. It may be possible for two or more people to produce a combined report for their folders.

Argument or discussion
Expressing a point of view needs careful planning and organisation. You may include in your folder an article from a book or magazine that you disagree with. You could write your response in the form of a letter. It is important to state your opinions calmly and logically.

Writing a play
Give the play a definite story line. Avoid long stage directions and try to make the dialogue sound real. The more characters you have, the more difficult it is to organise your play. Read your play aloud to yourself to see if it sounds real.

Poetry
Poetry is often the best way to express your feelings. Do not be concerned about rhyme. It is more important to find the right word than a rhyming one.

Planning your folio

Your coursework can be round a theme. Plan for variety whether it is or not. Scour newspapers for ideas and the unusual. If you are working round a theme plan it out. Here is a suggested plan for the theme: **Animals in the service of people**:

Story   Someone who ill-treats animals is paid back in some way. Life from the point of view of your dog. A planet where they have a different view of animals.
Description   Battery hen factory. Market scene when an animal due for slaughter escapes. Feeding the ducks in the park on Sunday.
Argument   Why you should become a vegetarian. Why we should protect all wildlife. Why crossbows should be banned.
Play   Some young people plan a raid on a laboratory where they experiment on animals. Their characters are shown as they plan the raid, what happens on the raid, and when they are questioned by the police.
Poetry   Your feelings about your pet. An old woman's feelings about her guide dog. Caught in a trap. Chimpanzee in a cage.
Evaluative   A survey on fox hunting.
Factual   Your own experiences of ill-treatment to animals and some possible laws to combat this.

Different styles

Each type of writing needs a different style. For instance, a set of instructions will probably be written in shorter sentences than a story about your experiences. Newspaper articles and advertisements have particular distinctive styles. Include some examples of each, trying to fit the style to the purpose. For instance, in an advert for radio you would include sound effects with the speech. Colour would be an important part of a poster advert.

Accuracy

There is little excuse for poor arrangement, paragraphing, spelling and punctuation in a piece of work you have had time to prepare. Re-draft your work, making additions or omissions, if necessary. Change the order of your points until you are satisfied you have produced the best effort you can.

List of authors

Page	Source	Author
20	*The Kitchen*	Arnold Wesker
36	*Inflation*	Dr Harold Priestley
47	*Journey through Love*	John Hillaby
49	*Fire*	Leonard Rule
65	*Hiroshima*	John Hersey
78	*The Scarecrows*	Robert Westhall
83	*A Rose for Winter*	Laurie Lee
97	*The Raffle*	V.S. Naipaul
103	*She's Leaving Home*	The Beatles
113	*Going Home*	Barry Hines
122	*Journey to Jo'burg*	Beverley Naidoo
125	*View of a Pig*	Ted Hughes
137	*Three Men in a Boat*	Jerome K Jerome
140	*The Duck Walk*	Keith Waterhouse
147	*The Midnight Fox*	Betsy Byars
148	*Kes*	Barry Hines
151	*Survival: South Atlantic*	Cindy Buxton Annie Price
160	*Very Nice, Very Nice*	Annette Tencha
162	*Tiger and the Rose*	Vernon Scannell

Extracts suitable for reading aloud

9	*Conversation with Mita*
12	*The talent*
20	*The kitchen*
36	*Inflation*
47	*Tracks*
49	*Factory fire*
65	*Hiroshima*
72	*The mugger*
78	*The mill*
81	*A frightening experience*
83	*A wedding party in Spain*
97	*The raffle*
103	*She's leaving home*
111	*Getting your own back*
113	*Going home*
122	*Journey to Jo'burg*
125	*View of a Pig*
125	*The Irish Pig*
140	*The duck-walk*
147	*Counting the wrinkles*
148	*Kes*
149	*Three men in a boat*
151	*Setting up camp*
160	*A frightening experience*
162	*A fateful time*
172	*A newspaper report favouring privatisation*
173	*A newspaper report opposing privatisation*